More Praise for This Boc

MW00990649

"Donnolo addresses quotas as the keystone to a total revenue approach for companies. Applying the principles of design thinking to this system leads to better results, more motivated teams, and less friction."

—David Kenny, CEO, Nielsen

"One of the realities of the modern sales organization is the fact that quotas are never fully solved. Companies eagerly spend untold millions to create plans and set quotas for reps . . . only to then throw them out shortly after putting them in place. Maybe it's time to consider a different approach. That's exactly what Mark Donnolo has done in this remarkable book. He tackles this seemingly intractable challenge by taking a completely different approach—one rooted in design thinking—to show how any organization can (and should) replace their current quota approach with one that actually does what it's designed to do: Motivate and engage all sellers to reach their highest levels of performance."

—Matt Dixon, Co-Author, *The Challenger Sale*
and *The Challenger Customer*

"This is a timely topic. Goal setting is an extremely challenging concept due to historical performance, opportunity, maturity, nature of services, broader market dynamics, and team sizes. This book incorporates all of these elements and finally helps you connect the art and science of quota setting."

—Rick Trainor, CEO, Business Services, LexisNexis Risk Solutions

"A brilliantly written book that eclipses all others. Instead of focusing only on the number, Donnolo challenges the thinking process of the sales leader. Sales Design Thinking is a revolutionary approach to solve the sales organization's real challenge by engaging both brain hemispheres. This book will help you solve your quota problem!"

—Gerhard Gschwandtner, CEO, Selling Power

"In this thorough guide, Mark Donnolo offers a step-by-step approach for bringing order to the chaos of quota setting. His novel application of design thinking to this thorny problem works to provide a coherent framework for structuring the quota setting effort, and to generate valuable insight for overcoming the many difficulties that make quota setting so challenging."

—Robert Kelly, Chairman, Sales Management Association

"*Quotas! Design Thinking to Solve Your Biggest Sales Challenge* provides today's sales managers with actionable strategies they can immediately use to help them set challenging sales quotas in a fast-paced, highly charged environment. Cleverly designed and written, it will provoke new thinking about quota-setting and quickly become the gold standard for the next generation of high-achieving sales organizations."

—Stephen J. Bistritz, EdD, Co-Author, *Selling to the C-Suite*

Quotas!

Design Thinking to Solve Your Biggest Sales Challenge

Mark Donnolo

© 2019 ASTD DBA the Association for Talent Development (ATD)
All rights reserved. Printed in the United States of America.
22 21 20 19   1 2 3 4 5

No part of this publication may be reproduced, distributed, or transmitted in any form or by any means, including photocopying, recording, information storage and retrieval systems, or other electronic or mechanical methods, without the prior written permission of the publisher, except in the case of brief quotations embodied in critical reviews and certain other noncommercial uses permitted by copyright law. For permission requests, please go to www.copyright.com, or contact Copyright Clearance Center (CCC), 222 Rosewood Drive, Danvers, MA 01923 (telephone: 978.750.8400; fax: 978.646.8600).

ATD Press is an internationally renowned source of insightful and practical information on talent development, training, and professional development.

ATD Press
1640 King Street
Alexandria, VA 22314 USA

Ordering information: Books published by ATD Press can be purchased by visiting ATD's website at www.td.org/books or by calling 800.628.2783 or 703.683.8100.

Library of Congress Control Number: 2019947587

ISBN-10: 1-95049-623-6
ISBN-13: 978-1-95049-623-5
e-ISBN: 978-1-95049-624-2

ATD Press Editorial Staff
Director: Sarah Halgas
Manager: Melissa Jones
Associate Director, Content: Justin Brusino
Developmental Editor: Kathryn Stafford
Production Editor: Hannah Sternberg
Text Design: Michelle Jose
Cover Design: Carl Cox

Printed by Data Reproductions Corporation, Auburn Hills, MI

To my mom, Christina Donnolo, who has always encouraged me to pursue my goals. She's still trying to figure out what I really do.

Contents

Introduction

It had been one of our busiest holiday seasons in years; now it was late spring and we weren't hitting our numbers. I was driving the team, but they seemed distracted and weren't getting results. Their attention was elsewhere. Over the past several months I had clicked through the checklist of options for building their capabilities. We had gone through some refresher training. I instructed, I demonstrated, and then I had them practice the activities that lead to success. We'd grown really close over six years. I was confident that Isabel and Olivia had the talent to meet the expectations I had for them. I had a lot invested in those two. They were loyal to the organization, and I hated the idea of giving them the sack. I preferred to develop them rather than trade them out. Not to mention, if I were to let them go, their mother would have been furious. While we were having dinner in the kitchen with our two daughters, she reminded me that this was no time for a coaching session because it was a school night.

Nevertheless, we had household work to allocate. Since the girls had recently turned six and eight, it was important that we have weekly objectives. I had created a scorecard with performance measures: cleaning the kitchen, making beds, feeding three cats and two dogs, brushing teeth. And I had an Allowance Incentive Program (the AIP as I branded it) tied to each measure on a weighted point system with accelerators for over-achievement. There was plenty of upside for making a few more beds and feeding a few more cats. I thought, "Maybe I'm setting their goals too high. I could use some benchmarks. Perhaps I could tap into a group of parents at school and get some comparable productivity numbers from

their kids, then calibrate our quotas to the 75th percentile of that group."
After a long internal struggle, I realized setting their goals and getting
them to perform was about more than the spreadsheets. It was also about
looking in the mirror and understanding my young daughters and their
capabilities. I know I'm not alone among parents who bring their work
home. Looking for the answer in the analytics and benchmarks can be
tempting for a sales leader, but, as I learned firsthand, quota setting is a
challenge that goes far beyond the numbers.

❖ ❖ ❖

In my 30 years of working with sales leaders, one of the biggest issues
I've seen year after year in company after company is setting effective
quotas. According to our research at SalesGlobe, 61 percent of companies say that setting and managing effective quotas is one of their top
three sales effectiveness challenges. Ineffective quota setting can limit
the company's ability to hit its business plan. Quota challenges can affect the ability of the sales organization to reach its goals and target
compensation, lead to higher turnover, hinder the company's ability to
attract top talent, and lower the sales organization's motivation. Quota
setting and management is a topic that is often discussed from board
rooms to the front line. However, most companies have yet to fully
solve the problem.

Sales leadership knows it has to give the sales organization a goal
each year that it might not be able to reach, and bridge the gap between
what the company wants and what reps can accomplish. And frontline
sales reps often end up with quotas they think are unfair or ridiculous
and that jeopardize their ability to make a living. Each year, the tension
and dysfunction continue. Many companies rationalize the problem and
continue on this path for years, never coming to a solution. Without a
solution, quota challenges continue in the form of company sales performance challenges through goal under-attainment, cost challenges from

sporadic rep performance that results in misalignment of pay with performance, and people challenges with recruiting and turnover problems. For companies dealing with quota challenges, these must be solved to ensure the long-term health of the business.

Few organizations understand how to set quotas that reflect real market opportunity and sales capacity with enough transparency to motivate the reps. For many organizations, setting effective quotas is elusive because they try to solve the quota problem with the same time-worn approaches or avoid the problem altogether. The sales organization continues to shoulder the burden of misallocated numbers that affect the sales team and the company. Rather than battling with who gets the number, solving the quota problem requires new thinking to break down the challenge into its components and apply a problem-solving approach that engages the organization.

This is a book about quotas. But more important, this is a book about problem solving for quotas. It would be easy to write down everything we have learned about quotas from every organization we've worked with, but it is far more valuable to lay out an approach to solving the quota problem that any organization can apply. This book addresses challenges that affect every company in nearly every country. It is for the C-suite, sales leadership, sales operations, and frontline sales. It addresses sales leaders' needs to set effective quotas as well as sales representatives' needs to get a fair quota for themselves. And it looks at quotas in a new light, beginning with understanding your quota challenge, the story behind it, and applying Sales Design Thinking™—a five-step, iterative problem-solving process—to solve it. To that end, I'll provide some design thinking methods specific to sales along with some guiding principles.

To provide insight for our problem solving, our team conducted research that included interviews, surveys, and work with more than 140 companies. From this research, we found that quota setting is one of the top sales effectiveness challenges for most companies. It is also the top sales compensation challenge for most companies. We found most companies struggle not only with the data but also with the people dynamics and processes required to effectively set and manage quotas. But most significantly, we found a pattern of success for companies that are effective with quotas that includes the interaction of people, market opportunity, and sales capacity. I've included the results of this research throughout the book as part of the overall narrative.

As managing partner of SalesGlobe, a sales effectiveness consulting firm that serves Global 1000 clients, I've worked through these challenges and methods with companies around the world. As a former designer, my natural approach is to use design thinking to take apart a problem, look at components in a different way, and come up with new alternatives to solving it.

Chapter 1 begins with a look at the trouble with quotas. Setting and managing quotas is one of the top sales effectiveness issues, along with creating an effective sales strategy and sales process, and I examine a number of the analytical and human facets of quota challenges.

In chapter 2, I look at Sales Design Thinking, a method I've used over the years that helps to reframe the problem and redefine the Challenge Question. We can then disaggregate that challenge and begin to solve for the components of the quota problem. Sales Design Thinking gets to the critical "why" behind the problem and enables us to come up with a range of divergent solutions rather than follow the same old path of what we've done before or what competitors are doing that may not solve the true problem.

With the foundation of Sales Design Thinking, we move into chapter 3, which is about understanding the story behind the problem. For a lot of people, this begins a whole new way of approaching quotas. By understanding the story, we can dig much deeper into the root causes that can suggest potential solutions. From the story, we can also create a solution vision that projects the characteristics a great solution may have.

In chapter 4, I describe the first of the three major components of the Quota Success Model: people. People are at the center of solving the quota problem because most quota challenges involve leadership or user issues around clear process or comprehension. I describe the different functions in the organization that are involved in quota setting as well as their type of involvement and the dynamics between those groups.

Chapter 5 examines the next major component of the Quota Success Model: understanding market opportunity. Market opportunity sets the stage for what's available to us within our addressable market. It's driven by factors such as the segments that we focus on, the products that we offer, and our macroeconomic environment.

To round out the Quota Success Model, in chapter 6 I dive into the workings of sales capacity. This often-overlooked component defines what your organization can accomplish in going after its market opportunity. Sales capacity is driven by factors including role definition, headcount, talent level, focus, and workload. By putting together the three components of people, market opportunity, and sales capacity, you have the framework to solve the quota problem for any organization.

In the next three chapters, I detail a range of options to consider in your problem-solving process. In chapter 7, I reflect on history as a quota method. While historical quota-setting methods alone don't provide the best solution for most companies in fast-forward mode, they can provide useful input when applied with other forward-looking indicators.

Sales potential methods are the subject of chapter 8. I describe methods that consider potential at the account level and at the market level, both with variations that are data robust and variations that work when accurate market data aren't readily available.

In chapter 9, I focus on account planning as a method for quotas. While account planning is usually used just for creating an action plan, it can also be a valuable source of detailed, account-specific information on multiyear and single-year goals.

With the quota solution finally developed, in chapter 10 I turn to the topic of making change. Organizations can easily miss the importance of well-planned and executed communications and change management when undertaking a transition as consequential as quota setting. In this chapter I look at articulating the "why" behind the change, understanding the organization's change readiness and capability, and creating your campaign.

Since I apply a question-based design thinking approach throughout the book, I include in the appendix my 10 favorite quota questions and analytics, Powerful Questions and Analytics for Understanding Your Story. These will give you insight as you begin your work.

I've truly enjoyed writing this book and providing some thinking on quota setting that you can apply to get new results. I hope that you find it valuable and that it puts you on a path of discovery on your quota problem-solving journey.

CHAPTER 1

The Trouble With Quotas

It was raining, which added to the mood of the dreary morning as my body reminded me that it was only 1:30 a.m. in the States. I swung open the door of the black cab and sprinted into Victoria Station to catch the 7:10 a.m. train. I had about an hour's ride, enough time to prepare for my meeting. Our client, a global network technology company, had been struggling to hit its numbers. Once a high flyer with double-digit annual growth, in recent years it had looked more like a plane going down.

I thought about how appropriate our meeting location was. The town of Aldershot tempers the typical charm that Americans feel when we visit the UK. Before the mid-19th century, the region was a desolate place with a small population. During the Crimean War, Aldershot found its purpose as a military town—and the rest is history. Stepping off the train that rain-soaked morning, the British Army barracks seemed to complement the corporate office parks that would be the scene of today's battle.

At the company's EMEA (Europe, the Middle East, and Africa) headquarters, we had to referee the face-off between Alan, the director of EMEA sales, and global headquarters back in New York, which had just levied a quota on the EMEA theater. The growth number, driven by finance, went far beyond what the EMEA sales leader thought was possible. "This looks like a goal from about seven years ago when the market was hot," Alan began. "We were the only theater that beat our number last year and what did we get rewarded with? A bigger quota! They have no idea what they're asking us to do. If we agree to this, I'll be made redundant by next year, guaranteed!" Alan was clearly heating up. He was looking for an out—for a way to push back on a number that was going to kill his team's motivation and its compensation.

Only a week earlier, I'd had a similar conversation in New York about the unrealistic expectations the company was putting on all its theaters worldwide. Finance was feeling pressure from the CEO, who was feeling pressure from investors. The company hadn't been performing like it had several years back due to factors that included heavier competition, more demanding customers, an increasingly saturated market, and an economy that had slowed. Nevertheless, the CEO had to have his number and finance was going to help him get it.

During the back and forth between headquarters, the Americas, EMEA, and Asia Pacific theater leaders—as well as the country leaders within the theaters—the conversations were all about the number. Everyone had taken a position in one of two camps: either "This is what we must have" or "Here is why we can't do what's being asked of us." And yet, as we put some deeper work into it with each of the leaders, we found that the answer wasn't the number. The answer was what went into the number. It was about the quota-setting approach, the assumptions, and the people. The company had grown accustomed to imposing a big number on the sales organization during the high-growth times. But as the market got tougher, this imposition only created disbelief, resentment, and underperformance in the sales organization.

Something had to change.

Quota Tension Points

Among the range of challenges we deal with in sales organizations, one keeps rising to the surface: setting effective quotas. In the simplest terms, quotas are the connection between the company's growth goal and the individual growth goal for each sales person. Without a quota, the sales person has no ownership of the larger company business plan and no accountability for their role in its success or failure.

Companies put a lot of time and energy into the development of their sales strategies and programs for the coming year. But when they get to the end of the planning and design cycle, close to the fourth quarter, they've used up so much of their time and resources that typically you'll hear, "OK, we're going to set quotas next week, and we'll be ready to go." They don't give it the attention needed.

Another challenge is that the players change with quota setting. Most sales program development involves the sales organization, the sales operations organization, human resources, and marketing. To some degree, the finance organization is also involved; they will be asked to validate the financials to ensure they're acceptable. But, when it comes to quota setting, finance tends to take a larger role. For many organizations, the number will come from the C-suite, supported by the board of directors and investors, and will be picked up by the finance organization—usually the CFO—and then presented, or pushed, to the sales organization. The sales organization is the recipient of a colossal sales quota expectation, which then has to be allocated to the sales teams, business units, theaters, regions, sales management, and front line.

The finance organization isn't traditionally oriented toward sales and may not be particularly knowledgeable about what sales does. It may even see the sales team as a necessary evil and sales compensation as an expense to manage and reduce. Obviously, this is not how the sales organization sees itself. Jana Schmidt, CEO of Harland Clarke, describes the relationship. "The two tension points are the sales team, who wants to have the lowest targets possible, and the finance team, who is looking for something fair, but something that is in alignment with helping the company really grow. Finance has a lot of visibility into how much you're paying people, and how much they are being paid for the results they're delivering. As leaders, we have to take the impartial and balanced view. Sales has to have a chance to be their best."

The Top Sales Effectiveness Challenges: Where Do Quotas Fit?

Of course, quota setting isn't a stand-alone practice. It interacts with a number of sales effectiveness disciplines. If these related disciplines aren't clearly defined or aligned, they can ripple into issues that show in poor organization quota attainment. Let's look at some of the other top sales effectiveness challenges and their connection to quotas cited in our survey by companies across industries (Figure 1-1).

Figure 1-1. The Top Sales Effectiveness Challenges

Developing an Actionable Sales Strategy

About half of the companies surveyed had challenges with translating business strategy into a sales strategy. When we talk about sales strategy, the conversations can get broad and complex. But, simply put, the sales strategy is just an action plan for the organization to achieve its sales goals. That action plan includes decisions around what types of markets and customers we'll target, our value proposition to each segment, and our coverage model, which includes the channels, roles, rules of engagement, and territories. All those decisions ultimately tie back to shaping the sales strategy and priorities around markets, offers, and financials from the chief sales officer through to each role that controls a piece of those priorities in direct sales, channel sales, and service.

Implementing an Effective Sales Process

Forty-five percent of companies see the sales process as a top challenge. Within the sales coverage model, the sales process defines how each role involved in originating, developing, and servicing customers and opportunities works and also how those roles work together. The sales process must be built to reflect the customer's buying process and deliver the desired customer experience (rather than becoming an internally driven process); key to this is defining the rules of engagement between roles. Mapping the roles and rules of engagement cleanly on paper doesn't mean that people will actually operate the same way. For example, the hand-off engagement point between a new business developer and a current account manager can vary dramatically depending on how long the business developer continues to receive quota credit for the new sale. Credit the business developer for all or most of the total contract value of the sale up front, and they'll be off to the next new customer opportunity. Space the quota crediting out for a year and they'll stay highly engaged with the account manager and customer to maximize their revenue quota credit. Establishing the right goals, and crediting for the performance measures each role controls, drives the right behaviors in the field.

Hiring and Retaining Top Talent

A-players are the lifeblood of any sales organization, but almost a third of companies see hiring and retaining top talent as a key challenge. The issues include understanding and defining the optimal capability profile for each role ("Are we hiring people with the right sales DNA for the job? Do we have the right inventory of DNA in our organization now? And if not, what are we doing about it?"), communicating the right employee value proposition to the market (including pay, job content, career path, culture, and company affiliation), and fulfilling that value proposition. Effective quotas play a role by providing realistic, market-based goals that are attainable with expected performance and can be overachieved with high performance.

Coaching and Developing the Team

For any sales strategy to be effective, the organization has to be disciplined about following the right practices and habits. Twenty-seven percent of companies are challenged with coaching and developing their teams, which is the teaching and reinforcement mechanism to convert strategy into consistent action and results. For many organizations, the practice of coaching is not formally taught to managers, who are expected to learn it through observation. As a result, coaching is a vulnerability point. Quotas should create goal congruence between levels in the sales organization from the front line through managers and directors, aligning them on the same priorities. Some types of goals for managers, such as having a targeted portion of their reps who reach their quotas, can highlight to managers the importance of coaching and developing their teams. To this point, in the average company, only about 42 percent of reps attain or exceed their quotas compared to the best practice of 50 percent to 70 percent, so there is a lot of opportunity for managers. Paired with leadership development programs, quotas can work as a coaching enabler.

Aligning Sales Compensation With the Strategy

Sales compensation is a hot topic for most companies and a top-three issue for about a quarter of them. The sales compensation plan connects the strategy to the actions of the sales organization and should represent the company goals that each role influences or controls. Sales compensation challenges include paying competitively, creating adequate upside opportunity to attract top performers, aligning pay mix and measures with each role, and keeping it all simple enough to communicate clearly and drive the right behaviors. Even the best sales compensation plan design that encapsulates all these elements will fall flat without effective quotas that link performance to pay.

Integrating Organizations From Mergers and Acquisitions

In economies both robust and lean, M&A presents companies with opportunities to create stronger, combined organizations. Since about half of our work at SalesGlobe is in M&A sales organization integrations, we see the challenges that go along with them. For the companies that cite this as an issue (about a quarter), following the vision that drove the merger or acquisition is difficult because bringing together two or more sales strategies, sales organization structures, sales talent pools, incentive compensation programs, and quota methodologies requires heavy lifting. On top of that, many organizations that are coming together don't have matching cultures. For example, merging two organizations—one with a strong sales culture and the other with a strong finance culture—can create conflict and ongoing resentment. Quotas that represent the integrated market opportunity and sales capacity of the combined organizations are critical to planning for and attaining the benefits originally envisioned with the merger or acquisition.

The Top Issues Behind Quota Setting

Contrary to what you might believe, quotas aren't all about the numbers, and the top quota challenges aren't all about the math. Quota problems are usually a combination of the people, the process, and the analytics. If you're all about the numbers, it's time to look at your people and process skills. It generally takes a cross-functional effort between sales, finance, operations, marketing, and senior leadership to define and operate the right quota-setting approach. And because finance tends to take a prominent role in quota setting (switching places with sales, which usually leads the sales compensation design), the organizational dynamics change. We'll explore more about these roles in chapter 4.

First, let's take a deeper look at some of the top issues behind quota setting (Figure 1-2):

- history doesn't predict the future
- reconciling bottom-up input
- not considering sales capacity
- driven by finance
- data gaps
- missing market opportunity
- no belief in the process.

Figure 1-2. The Top Quota Challenges

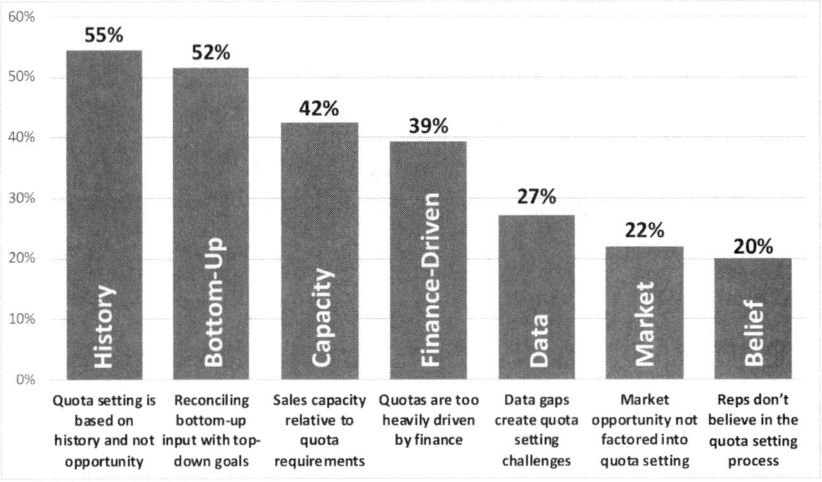

Quota setting is based on history and not opportunity — History — 55%
Reconciling bottom-up input with top-down goals — Bottom-Up — 52%
Sales capacity relative to quota requirements — Capacity — 42%
Quotas are too heavily driven by finance — Finance-Driven — 39%
Data gaps create quota setting challenges — Data — 27%
Market opportunity not factored into quota setting — Market — 22%
Reps don't believe in the quota setting process — Belief — 20%

Quota Qualm: Do Quotas Demotivate Cabbies?

Why is it harder to catch a taxicab in New York City on a rainy day than on a sunny day? You're probably thinking, "That's easy. Because more people ride cabs when it rains." The problem is one of demand. Right? Well, it turns out that it's actually a problem of supply too. According to researchers from Carnegie Mellon and the University of Chicago, when it rains, cabbies tend to meet their daily quotas faster—and then they go home. Apparently, they may not be motivated to do much more than meet their quota. Not only are there more riders on rainy days, but there are also fewer cabs! A *Harvard Business Review* paper looked at the phenomenon and commented, "If NYC taxi drivers used a longer time horizon (perhaps weekly or monthly), kept track of indicators of increased demand (e.g., rain or special events), and ignored their typical daily goal, they could increase their overall wages, decrease the overall time they spend working, and improve the welfare of drenched New Yorkers." When you put hard end-points on quotas, such as days, months, or quarters, you tend to get gaming behaviors to determine whether to keep selling or to push demand to the next period, like the cabbies. Give your organization the right timing and enough upside earning potential to keep them achieving beyond the quota.

History Doesn't Predict the Future

Many companies use history as a predictor of the future, mostly because it's easy to do and it seems logical. Sixty-five percent of companies in our survey use historical quota-setting methods for at least one of their sales channels, and 55 percent of companies also see the limitations of historical methods as a top quota challenge. This method causes us to look in the rear-view mirror to set our goals for the future. The typical historical approach takes the sales representative's performance, looking either at the past growth rate or the growth rate over a period of years, and applies this to where they stand right now. If a rep sold $5 million and historically grew their account base by 10 percent annually, we might simply apply that 10 percent to the $5 million, and that number would be an approximation of next year's activity.

One of the issues here is that history creates the situation where, if you did well, you're probably going to get a quota increase, and if you didn't do well, you'll get a smaller goal based on your historical performance.

Here's a real-life example of this very situation: A retirement services company we worked with was heavily focused on historical quota setting. This typically resulted in a single number, which could be well defended by history, but not necessarily by changes in the company or the market. There were frequent arguments about the number's accuracy—and even fights breaking out among the sales team and management. As we helped them to break the number apart and build it up again, they began to see that history was just one component of quota setting. There were other indicators of potential as well, such as the number of people employed by the customer organization who need retirement services and various industry data around market opportunity. They broke down those indicators and layered their new understanding on top of the historical data. Soon, sales and management were having conversations about all the indicators of potential, not just the historical numbers. This company didn't have to abandon its favorite method. But it did begin to see history as a first phase to help them on their journey.

Reconciling Bottom-Up Input

Usually, the big goals for the business are established by senior leadership and then allocated to the organization. As you'll see in chapter 5, these top-down goals should incorporate bottom-up intelligence either in establishing the overall goal or in calibrating the allocation of quotas across the organization to increase the accuracy of quotas. Bottom-up input can be a valuable method for building effective quotas, but it's not always realistic. According to Todd Abbott, executive vice president of sales and marketing at global telecommunications giant Mitel, "Bottom-up is not practical in a transactional business. It makes much more sense when your business is installed-base and large accounts with a long sales cycle." He concludes, "So, it really depends on the business, and what the mix of the business is." In about 52 percent of companies, reconciling input from the bottom up and top down is a key quota issue, which can involve a lack of reconciliation process and a lack of reliable field-level data on the market or sales capacity.

Not Considering Sales Capacity

Forty-two percent of organizations describe challenges with incorporating sales capacity into quota setting. Sales capacity, as we'll see in chapter 6, counterbalances market opportunity to identify what the sales organization is capable of producing. Sales capacity considers obvious factors such as headcount and average productivity for each role. Below that, sales capacity is driven by factors that include focus of sales time, sales workload, close rates, and talent.

Driven by Finance

Thirty-nine percent of companies point the finger at finance. Before any finance readers get defensive, most executives that we interviewed and have worked with over the years acknowledge the critical role finance plays in driving sales planning and quota setting. But many also describe a need for finance to become more market sensitive by aligning with the sales and marketing organizations to better understand market segments, customers, and sales capacity. It sounds like finance has an open invitation in most companies to conduct some customer sales call ride-alongs with the reps. We'll look at the people aspect of quota setting in chapter 4.

Data Gaps

Data is a top challenge for 27 percent of companies. We hear comments like, "We just don't have forward-looking information on the market, our customers, our product trends, or growth rates, so we can't set goals that consider future opportunities." This was a great excuse years ago, but with the proliferation of information available about companies, markets, and purchasing indicators, we are now data rich and information poor. Most companies have an abundance of data but don't know what to do with it. They don't leverage it to get usable, valuable insight, which they could then apply to sales planning and quota setting.

Teams amass terabytes of data, then begin the process of data cleansing, matching, and alignment from multiple databases. They look at the data and pronounce it garbage. "But it's missing information for data fields," they declare. "There's no employee count, no purchase history—and I'm not sure the information's believable." Pretty soon, the exercise becomes an extended data improvement project rather than a way to capture some useful information for making logic-based assumptions. Coupled with the "garbage data trap" is data paralysis, where the team is hypnotized by complexity. Rather than simplifying the approach and looking for the major elements and themes that will help the organization move ahead, the team spins in an endless loop of complexity. Meanwhile, everyone else quietly steps away and goes back to the old methods.

Missing Market Opportunity

About 22 percent of companies are challenged with incorporating market opportunity in quota setting. As I mentioned, market opportunity sits opposite sales capacity in a balanced approach to quotas. While market opportunity estimation may conjure images of data-intensive sales potential estimation, there are a number of ways to approach it, from applying market modifiers to territory information to conducting pipeline estimates to full-out market heat mapping. The key to incorporating market opportunity into quota setting is to find a method that's understood and accepted by the organization, simple enough to scale, and accurate enough to represent the opportunities in and differences between territories. We'll delve into some market opportunity methods in chapters 7 and 8.

No Belief in the Process

Sometimes quota setting is conducted in a rudimentary way or lacks a clear process. Management may take a big number, spread it across the organization (in what's known as the peanut butter method), and allocate it down to each level in the same way. It's more of a fill-in-the-blank exercise than thoughtful planning; unfortunately, it can result in a lack of belief in the process, cited by about 20 percent of companies.

We worked with a leading wireless telecom company that had an approach few believed in and an apparent lack of process. Its method was to look at historical information and then spread the quota across the markets without regard to the variations in the markets. Then they allowed managers to respond by registering exceptions to these goals, stating why they couldn't be achieved. On the surface, there appeared to be little process and little trust. But upon further examination we discovered a back-and-forth string of emails between finance, sales leaders, and sales management that showed signs that there was an actual process supported by undocumented institutional knowledge. Once we found it, we formalized it, made it more market based, and communicated it. The organization was able to mobilize around that process because they finally could see it and understand it. After a few successful operating cycles, they began to believe in it.

Quotas are psychological as well as analytical. If I think that the quota I've been given is unrealistic or too challenging, I might not take ownership of it because it was just handed to me. However, if I believe in the process, if I'm engaged in it, and if I understand how that process works, the psychology will be different: I'll see the quota as more attainable, and my chances of reaching it become greater. Even if the sales reps aren't directly involved, their belief in the process's integrity and its fairness is essential to their ownership of their quota.

Five Points to Consider

For most companies, quota setting is one of the biggest challenges that, when faced, often leads to a number of sub-challenges. On the one hand, take comfort in knowing that you're not alone. You share the pain with a lot of other great organizations. On the other hand, that doesn't help you solve the problem. It also doesn't help you understand your own company's issues or its root causes. In order for us to begin the journey of effective quota setting and attaining those quotas, you have to start with some self-reflection as a business—understanding what your issues are around quota setting. In the next chapter, we'll talk about how to identify your problem and see how it evolved over time, so that you can diagnose the root causes and build the right solution for your business. In the meantime, here are five points to consider:

- Quota challenges often are not stand-alone issues but are connected with other sales effectiveness issues.
- To better understand your quota issue, determine whether it is related to a misalignment in upstream disciplines like clear sales strategy, sales process, or sales role definition.
- Look at how your quota issue may be related to other enablement disciplines that include sales compensation, sales talent, or supporting technology.
- Don't assume that your quota issue is about the numbers. Look at the people and process parts of quota setting and quota management.
- If your organization is struggling to set and achieve quotas, it may be attributable to a lack of method, process, or engagement of the organization.

CHAPTER 2

Sales Design Thinking to Solve Your Quota Problem

I climbed the subway stairs, transitioning from the cool, dank odor of the Seventh Avenue line into the sunlight and fresh exhaust of a sweltering May afternoon in New York. It was 1980-something, and I was in the middle of my design school education, excited about my first internship in the city—which I actually still needed to land. We didn't have the Internet. We didn't even have email. Back then, the practice was to send letters with résumés to prospective employers and hope they would read them and give you an opportunity to have a portfolio review. That was what designers called a first interview. If you were coming into the city from another location—Philadelphia, in my case—you could schedule some appointments ahead of time. But there were those coveted design firms that wouldn't respond to your letters. To fill in the open spots on the schedule, you'd get on a pay phone—no cell phones either—and dial up a few local firms, refer to the letter you sent and the professor who had referred you to that well-known design director, and mention that you were just down the street and had a few minutes available for a meeting. If you were lucky, you'd get a portfolio review with a design director in a great firm, they'd give you a critique, and maybe you'd get a follow-up appointment for a real interview, then maybe—maybe—an internship.

I stood with my portfolio between my knees, crammed in a phone booth at the edge of Madison Square Park on East 26th Street. I was working through my list of calls and got to a firm called Chermayeff & Geismar. They were at the pinnacle of the corporate identity field, having designed trademarks and branding campaigns for clients like Chase Manhattan, Mobil, NBC, and PBS. Getting an internship there would be the ultimate. I had a referral from my professor to one of the partners of the firm, Steff Geissbuhler. Of course, Steff hadn't responded. I'm sure he was too busy and had hundreds of design students like me clamoring for an opportunity. I made the call, recited my script (the delivery of which I had perfected through numerous calls) and waited to hear that Steff was out of the country, or that he was with a client, or that, honestly, he had absolutely no time or interest in talking to another student like me. "Yes, Mr. Geissbuhler has a spot at 3 p.m."

"What?" I replied. "Uh . . . well I think that would work for me. I'm just down the street so I can be there shortly." It was about 2:45. I happened to be camped out across the street from their offices on the park, so I walked calmly through traffic and was there at 2:48.

After waiting a while in the lobby conference room, my portfolio on the table, I saw Steff enter, dressed smartly in black, sporting a full mustache and looking the part. He greeted me warmly. He didn't know me but knew my professors, so he assumed I was worth a few minutes of his time.

I paged through my portfolio slowly. At first, he stared quietly. Then he asked me to turn back a page. "He must like that project," I thought. In his crisp Swiss-German accent he said, "Tell me about this one." I thought it was a good-looking piece, a trademark I had designed for a school project. I told him about the project and my design. "What was the problem you were trying to solve?" he asked. I explained the objectives of the project. He squinted. "What was your design concept?

How does the solution you developed solve the problem?" I explained the idea behind my good-looking solution.

He twirled the tip of his moustache between his fingers. He was silent. He flipped to another page and asked, "For this one . . . what other options did you consider? Take me through your thought process." The room was beginning to heat up. The walls were moving closer. I felt intellectually barren. I continued to answer as Steff continued with a few more questions and my answers began to spiral along with the portfolio review.

Steff Geissbuhler. François Robert Photography

Finally, he stopped and turned the conversation. Steff gave me a few sage words about the problem and the idea and about the value of design not being in its appearance but in the strength of its concept and effectiveness at solving the problem. There's an abundance of attractive design in the world but a dearth of design that solves the real problem. About 15 painful minutes later, he thanked me for stopping by and asked me to give his regards to my professors. I left the office briskly, stunned and a little confused. About a day later, I began to sense the lesson. Nearly 40 years from that day, as you now know, I still remember it. It has helped shape my thinking ever since. The work we do (whether design or business) is not about getting to a result. It's about understanding, exploring, and solving the problem.

A few years ago, when I served on the board of trustees of the design school I had attended in Philadelphia, I talked with Steff again. I recounted the story and told him how valuable the lesson had been to me. He smiled. I don't think he remembered.

Design Thinking for Sales

As we saw in the last chapter, there's no shortage of challenges around quota setting and— more broadly—sales effectiveness. For a sales problem solver, it's an abundant playground with a potentially big upside for the organization. When solving sales problems, organizations face a number of issues:

Looking at the problem myopically, like it can be solved independently. Quotas support decisions in related upstream disciplines like sales strategy and sales coverage. So, problems usually need to be solved in concert with other disciplines, such as account segmentation, sales role design, sales process, or territory design, to make sure they all align.

Using approaches they've used previously or found somewhere else. Rather than working through a problem-solving approach and creating a solution that's right for the company and the situation, they replicate old methods and apply them as a solution to a problem where they may not fit.

Expecting that benchmarks will provide an answer. Sure, understanding how competitors perform or how they've addressed a similar problem is useful for reference. But those metrics and benchmarks are most useful for context, not as a solution to the organization's specific problem.

In the introduction of this book, I mentioned that it's critical to ask "why" before jumping to an answer. The first whys are: Why would we replicate something we've done before, follow the lead of someone on the team who did it that way in their previous company, or copy competitors and miss the opportunity to create a solution that gives us an advantage in our market? The next whys are: Why are we dealing with this quota problem, why do we want to solve it, and why might there be a better answer?

We need a method to help solve our quota problem. The method I propose is a time-tested approach for creative problem solving. From the start of my career in the design world, I used creative approaches and principles in my work in corporate identity, branding, and communications design. After my design career, I worked for years with major companies on complex sales effectiveness issues. As I wrestled with solving these problems with executives, I realized the value of design thinking and combining the left brain (analytical) with right brain (creative) processes to solve sales problems. With our team at SalesGlobe, we developed powerful creative problem-solving approaches that we use with sales leaders to help them come up with new ideas. These ideas result in actionable programs that ultimately give their organizations the strategic and financial results they're looking for. I detailed some of these in my book *The Innovative Sale.*

In the world of design and engineering, design thinking is a five-step process that begins with empathizing with those who face the problem you want to solve. When you can understand their problem, you're ready for step two: defining the problem. Next comes ideation—brainstorming—where team members share ideas for a solution. Then you build and test a prototype. However, the steps are not linear. You're always checking in with the stakeholders affected by the problem. It's an iterative process—back and forth, with some tinkering to get it right.

For the purpose of solving sales and quota problems, I'll give you some Sales Design Thinking methods as well as a few guiding principles. In the chapters that follow, I'll demonstrate these, starting with defining the problem and creating an insightful Challenge Question. Then we'll move on to some quota design frameworks and methods to prompt creative thinking. And we'll wrap up with ideas on quota communications and change management. My goal in all of this is to help you start to think differently, not only about problem solving for quotas but also about problem solving for your organization overall. You'll find that if you apply these Sales Design Thinking methods, you'll come up with more in-depth insight on the problem you're solving, and you'll unearth a broader range of solutions that will seed your final answer. With practice with your team, you'll also build these Sales Design Thinking methods into your creative muscle memory and begin thinking in a design frame of mind more naturally.

Let's look at some of the fundamentals of Sales Design Thinking that you can apply to quota setting. The good news is that you already know where to start: with the problem. Fill in the blank: Your organization has a quota-setting problem because _____. Whatever you wrote is probably just the surface problem. There's likely a lot more behind that. Here are five major steps in the Sales Design Thinking Process that can help you redefine and solve that problem (Figure 2-1).

Sales Design Thinking Step #1: Articulate the Problem Statement

For most organizations, articulating this is pretty easy because it's the thing the team has been talking about for months. Typically, it goes something like this:

"We need to fix the quota process because the sales team is underperforming."

If we try to solve for that problem statement, we may have our sights set on those specific points (quotas and team underperformance), attempt to fix only those ailments, and miss the underlying causes or related issues that also have to be fixed to address the whole quota problem. Pursuing the initial problem statement is the first mistake most organizations make. It's one of the reasons the problem doesn't go away and why other related problems emerge, such as lack of understanding and lack of adoption by the organization.

Figure 2-1. Sales Design Thinking Process

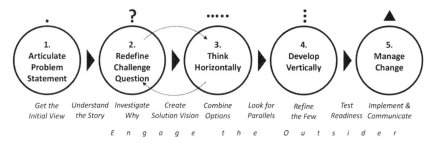

Sales Design Thinking Step #2: Redefine the Challenge Question by Understanding the Story

The problem statement is the starting point. To get beyond that initial view, we must first redefine the problem by understanding the story behind the problem. You may be thinking, "The story? I already know the story." The fact is, you likely know only a piece of the story—the piece that you can see from your perspective. Understanding the *whole* story gives us a new view on the problem and a more enlightened picture of what we need to solve for and what success looks like. Understanding the story behind the problem includes asking what the pain points are, how and when they developed, who was involved, why it was done the way it was done, and where it was happening. We'll discuss this in more detail in chapter 3. Working like a design detective to build out the story will reveal dimension and granularity on the problem that you wouldn't otherwise have. Apply the exercise on understanding the story in chapter 3 to your situation and you'll see.

With the story told, we then turn to asking the same types of questions to create a vision that describes what a successful outcome might look like. The solution vision doesn't give us the answer. It gives us a vision of how the answer could work. We ask what a successful outcome would be, how and when it could happen, who should be involved, why it would be beneficial or resisted, and where it should happen. With the story and solution vision, we then use the key parts of the solution vision to redefine the problem in the form of a Challenge Question. A Challenge Question has energy because a question about the challenge prompts continued thinking rather than simply a statement of the problem. The Challenge Question also has more dimension to it. For example, the problem statement,

> *"We need to fix the quota process because the sales team is underperforming."*

might be redefined this way:

> *"How do we fix the quota process for global accounts by engaging the theater sales leaders and aligning to new account assignments to increase the percentage of reps attaining quota and decrease rep turnover?"*

Wow! Suddenly the Challenge Question gives us a lot more to dig into. It's a starting point for a more targeted solution. At SalesGlobe, when we generate ideas for solving a client problem, we'll lay out the problem statement as a first step; then we write down one, two, or three Challenge Questions that we derive from the problem statement before we begin talking about ideas for the solution. It gives us clarity and granularity around the open questions we need to answer. And it makes the next step, horizontal thinking, more effective. In the next chapter, we'll begin with the problem statement, problem redefinition, and creating the Challenge Question.

Sales Design Thinking Step #3:
Think Horizontally and Combine Parallels

If you're an analytical thinker, we're going to go a little off road at this point by pushing right brain creative thinking. So put your mind into creative problem-solving mode. When most organizations work on solving for a problem statement, they usually have some initial ideas, then consider a limited set of options. They may begin developing those options as potential solutions. On occasion, if they are particularly motivated and have time away from all the urgent issues, the team might book a few hours for a meeting. They'll go offsite to free up their thinking. They'll load up their flip charts, whiteboards, and jumbo-sized sticky notes. They'll bring their colored markers. They'll call this *brainstorming*. But, in reality, they all probably enter the room with preconceived ideas about what the solution might be. And their ideas are probably ideas they've used before, seen others use, or heard about others using.

Instead of brainstorming, the team members spend most of their time making sure some of their ideas make it onto one of the flip charts, whiteboards, or sticky notes while supporting similar ideas from other team members. After investing a few hours in this activity, one lucky meeting attendee is handed all the flip charts, sticky notes, and whiteboard photos to turn them into a set of slides to distribute to the team. The team then starts working on how to develop and implement the best ideas. Although they might not be aware of it, the team has hit what I call an innovation roadblock. They've stayed within the realm of what they know and what's safe and understandable. Rather than looking at the initial brainstorming as flushing the creative pipes of preconceived ideas to make room for actual problem solving, they rush toward a solution. It's not because they aren't good problem solvers. It's not because they're devoid of ideas. When teams limit their thinking and hit an innovation roadblock, it's usually because:

They lack a problem-solving method. The team is familiar with this brainstorming activity and does it the way they learned it from generations of others who have kept their creative sights low. They never learned a better method for solving problems, so they just approach it intuitively.

They use a veneer of innovation. Like most teams, they work in an organization that uses various derivations of the word "innovation" to describe their mission, what they do, and how they think. The word shows up in their meetings, in their decks, and even in their annual reports. When they participate in innovation meetings, they get to dress casually, meet in unorthodox environments, interact with oversized toys, eat candy, and conduct team exercises to get them to think outside the box, the nine dots, or the latest creative constraint. But "innovation" is just a veneer over their normal ways of going about business. They don't actually know why they're trying to be innovative or how to innovate, which is why nothing about how they solve problems changes. They haven't made the transition to what I refer to as functional creativity, which is about solving a problem with specific objectives and constraints.

They stop short of discovery. Many executives are experts at what they do and aren't comfortable moving into the unknown. When teams exhaust their initial brainstorming and hit an innovation roadblock, they retreat to their areas of expertise rather than push further to see how their ideas will develop. But true problem solving often requires the team to get lost in discovery, to churn up ideas or fragments of ideas that can be combined and refined into new solutions.

When using Sales Design Thinking, instead of brainstorming ideas for solutions, we begin by brainstorming the Challenge Question and expanding the possibilities. We need a method to get us beyond our normal thinking patterns and our tendency to gravitate to the familiar. In horizontal thinking, we take a couple steps:

Disaggregate the Challenge Question. We take the Challenge Question and look for some of the key points we're solving for. This is an iterative process, so pick a couple or a few, develop them, and then try others. For example, let's take the Challenge Question from earlier:

> *"How do we fix the quota process for global accounts by engaging the theater sales leaders and aligning to new account assignments to increase the percentage of reps attaining quota and decrease rep turnover?"*

There are some key points to the Challenge Question that are worth exploring. For example: "engaging the theater sales leaders" and "new account assignments." We picked those because we suspected that getting the support of the sales leaders would be vital, and we also suspected that the new account assignments would be an important underpinning to improving the quota process. Let's start with exploring these two parts of the Challenge Question. Then we can look at other parts of the Challenge Question for additional ideas.

Explore meaning and options for key points of the Challenge Question. The idea here is to expand and explore how we might address each of these key components. For example, if we take "engaging the theater leaders" and "new account assignments," we would look at what those mean for global accounts. This is the brainstorming part because we collaborate as a team to explore each component.

When exploring each of these key points, we want to know what each one means and whether there are alternatives to it. There may be other questions as well. If we keep the conversation around each point flowing and natural rather than mechanical, we'll automatically start to generate questions and ideas about how to look at each component of the problem differently. The free-flowing iteration with the team will generate an abundance of ideas. It's important not to edit the outputs as you're going; just let them flow. You can trim them back and pull out the thought-provoking ideas later. It's also important not to stifle the conversation's flow with a lot of structure. For example, with the component "engaging the theater leaders," simply structure the conversation around questions such as:

- What do we know about the theater leaders?
- What is quality engagement with the theater leaders and leaders in general?
- What is engagement outside of this context?
- What are examples of how we've engaged with any theater leaders successfully or unsuccessfully?
- How can we engage and motivate theater sales leaders to have their country level reps support global accounts if they don't get adequate credit for those accounts?
- What issues do theater sales leaders have since global accounts were removed from their theaters and countries and moved to a global account organization?
- How do we need to engage others like sales leadership at the country and region level?
- What level of resistance to change is there by theater and country?
- Are there supporters of the global account program?
- How can we enlist them and educate others to get the same benefits?

For "account assignments" we could explore questions such as:

- What is an account assignment for global accounts?

- What changed about account assignments with the new approach?
- What challenges have we had with global account assignments?
- Are global account assignments for the whole account globally, the parts of the account at a country level, or some other definition?
- How do theater-leader assignments and crediting align with the total global account?
- How do country sales leader assignments and crediting align with each theater sales leader and total global account?
- How do global account assignments and crediting align with country-level P&L measurement?
- Do the account assignment and country-level P&L measures align or conflict?
- How should quota crediting align with how assigned accounts make decisions as either a global purchase decision, a global approved vendor status and hunting license, a local country-level decision, or some combination?
- How have global account customers responded to how we align our team to global accounts, and has crediting affected how the team interacts with those customers?

Those two components will generate an array of questions that will spur possible ideas around the solution, and the list of possible questions could continue. Let's look at a few examples of how combining components can lead to a solution.

Combine the options from each component. As we brainstorm meanings and options for the components, the team will churn up numerous questions and ideas about how to address that component. We can explore those ideas by themselves and come up with options. But we can also use a powerful technique of taking the individual components and reassembling them and testing them in combinations. For example, with the two previously mentioned, "engaging the theater leaders" and "account assignments," we might look at options such as:

- Aligning theater sales leader crediting with the revenue their accounts generate in their theaters as well as the revenue those accounts generate globally to motivate them to look beyond their theaters at the global potential of their accounts.

- Creating quota crediting for theater sales leaders that rewards them for a higher percentage of their reps reaching their global account quotas in addition to their country-level accounts.

- Developing a compelling value proposition for the global account program aimed toward further engaging theater sales leaders and country sales leaders.

- Enlisting the support of theater sales leaders who are proponents of the program to help win over all of the managers globally.

- Training country and region leaders, who report to the theater leaders, on how to develop bottom-up estimates of sales potential in their global accounts to give them input to and ownership of the quota-setting process.

- Developing a recurring communications campaign for the theater sales leaders and country sales leaders to regularly reinforce messages about the global account program and the benefits to them.

As the team begins to combine questions and ideas for each component, it will create an abundance of horizontal options. Their challenge, rather than trying to think of ideas, will be to pare down and prune ideas to the handful that are most realistic. Even some of the most radical ideas may have components or concepts that can be applied to more conservative options.

Look for parallels. With each new horizontal option, ask the question: "How do other organizations in our industry, outside of our industry, or outside of business approach this?" The idea is not to replicate solutions at this point but to look for parallel examples for how other organizations, especially outside of our industry, address that specific component and determine if there are ideas for that component that can be transferred to our business. For example, if we look at the component of "enlisting the support of theater sales leaders who are proponents of the program to help win over all of the managers globally" we may see examples of how organizations build membership of groups that can influence the larger team. We may look at global organizations in other industries that have been successful with global leaders to see how they do it. Do they build cross-theater teams that have common interests? Do they give additional leadership responsibility to the heads of those global councils?

You'll notice that through this method we can create a full range of horizontal or divergent thinking options. Some will be great ideas we wouldn't have thought about without this method. Of course, some might not make a lot of sense, and some will be pretty radical. You'll also notice that the ideas (such as enlisting the support of theater sales leaders who are proponents of the program) will go beyond quota setting to the disciplines and enablers that will make the quota setting solution more successful.

Quota Qualm: When Can We Know When to Say No?

Quotas aren't only for sales and production. They're the stuff of great literature and drama as well. Arthur Miller's classic play *All My Sons* revolves around Joe Keller, a factory owner whose business partner went to prison because he knowingly dispatched a shipment of defective cylinder heads to the military during World War II. His ethical lapse resulted in the deaths of 21 airmen. What led to this reckless and criminal behavior? The military was demanding shipments, and the partners thought their company's very existence was on the line. Keller had spent his life building the business, which he planned to turn over to his son Chris. Too afraid to admit there was a material defect, his partner made a ghastly executive decision to cover up the cracks and ship the cylinders. Keller, meanwhile, feigned the flu and stayed home that day. As a consequence of cowardice and moral failure, 21 airmen died, one man went to prison, and two families were devastated. While not all requirements are as dramatic or as dire as the one in *All My Sons,* the play serves as a moral lesson, a reminder that when the stakes are high, standing up to unreasonable demands is the right thing to do. Whether you're in the C-suite or on the front line, whether you've set the goal or received the goal from above, follow your ethical compass first.

Sales Design Thinking Step #4: Develop Vertically

After we've developed a range of options, we'll boil them down to a limited number according to criteria such as effectiveness with addressing the overall Challenge Question, degree of change, ease of implementation, and cost of implementation. With the preferred few options identified, it's time to move into vertical development. We're merging back into the lane where the team would have begun developing options after the old brainstorming approach. But now we're miles ahead. We have the benefit of having gone through the discovery steps of understanding the story, redefining the Challenge Question, and thinking horizontally.

We'll have ideas and possibilities to work with that we wouldn't have generated out of the old brainstorming approach. With vertical development, we turn each of the preferred options into a proposed solution. Usually we'll carry two or three of these through to the proposed solution stage. We want to have a limited number so we can concentrate our efforts, but we also want a range so we can compare options and, if necessary, anchor our preferred ideas among the other options. With the anchoring technique, instead of proposing one option to the leadership team, to which they respond either positively or negatively, we give them a range with our preferred option anchored in the middle. If we have two or three options, we can run the range from more conservative to moderate and to more extreme. Then the team can respond to each and gravitate toward one. If we're recommending the moderate option, that can be anchored by the more conservative (too little change) and extreme (too much change), making the moderate change easier to move to. Of course, if we need a significant change, we can move toward the more extreme.

A client of ours, the head of sales operations for a major communications company, makes a practice of anchoring and playing the extremes when her team proposes design options to the senior executive team. "We usually show three or four options with a recommended option somewhere in the middle," she told me. "The executives will invariably move toward the middle. But then a funny thing happens. They'll look at the radical options while they're considering the group. And then in our next meeting, one of them will suggest an idea that was part of one of the radical options, speaking like it's actually his idea, and will want to consider that as part of our final recommendation. So, we have our own way of subtly innovating within our conservative culture."

Sales Design Thinking Step #5: Manage Change

We've developed a great quota approach and it's going to make a real difference for the organization. But, just because we've developed a process and method on paper and we've been able to spreadsheet it out doesn't mean it's going to work in action. A couple of years ago, I met with a sales leadership team that had developed a pretty nice, straightforward, and practical quota solution. When I talked with them a few months later, I asked how the new approach was working. They explained that while they thought it would be easy to understand, the organization didn't get it and they reverted back to the old process. I asked them how they had rolled out the process. "We made an announcement and sent the process out to all of the managers with the dates for each milestone." That was it. They made one announcement. The organization didn't see the value in it. No one bought in, no one owned it—and it died on the vine.

With the new quota approach developed, we have to plan, communicate, and manage the change to get the results we're looking for. In chapter 10, we'll get into understanding the organization's tolerance for change, determining its capability to change, and developing an effective implementation and communications campaign.

The Magic of the Outsider

Ultimately, people are the center of the solution development process. The core members of your design team collaborate to identify the challenges, redefine them, and create the options. In chapter 4, we'll explore the players on the court. However, right now, there is one important role to incorporate, and it goes beyond the functions of sales, sales operations, finance, marketing, operations, and human resources: It's the role of the Outsider.

Anyone in any function can play the Outsider role, as long as they are knowledgeable about the subject of quota setting and they understand the organization and its issues. But the Outsider should come from outside the core design team and bring fresh perspective at key points in the process. For example, during horizontal thinking, the Outsider may join the team for a review of the Challenge Question and options. With a clear view on the situation the Outsider can ask questions, challenge ideas, and suggest options the team might consider.

Typically, in problem-solving situations, we fear the Outsider. You've been working hard, head down, investing time in developing solutions. Then an associate or your boss or your boss's boss walks by your desk or stops into your team meeting and asks, "Hey, what are you working on?" or "How's that project coming along?" or "Can I take a look at what you've come up with so far?"

You pause. The back of your neck tightens involuntarily. You've been working on this project for weeks. You've sacrificed your weekends. You're focused on closing this thing out. "What does he know about what we're doing?" "He's just gonna start asking uninformed questions and take us off track. Then I'm going to have to follow up on what he asks me." "I've got a deadline to hit for cryin' out loud!" You don't need this interruption.

Well, it's exactly what you and your team do need. In the solution development process, we necessarily get so close to our work that we can lose perspective and become myopically focused on our path. The Outsider provides that sometimes painful but always valuable interjection of reality. The Outsider asks questions that test our solutions. Because they haven't been deep in the process like our team has been, the Outsider will ask questions we've stopped asking. They may take us from our vertical, convergent thinking back to divergent thinking. Or they may confirm that we're on a good track.

On our team, we have meetings we call Brain Trusts (borrowed from FDR's New Deal). When one of our team is deep into a project, they can call a Brain Trust meeting at any point and invite any person or small group of people in the firm. We look forward to our Brain Trust meetings because they generate a special energy around the challenge and potential solutions. In the Brain Trust meeting the project team poses the Challenge Question. They walk through the key components of the Challenge Question they explored, then share their horizontal thinking with the Outsider. Then they stop. The interaction begins with the Outsider questioning, exploring, confirming, and suggesting with the team. We engage in our Brain Trust meetings passionately because they're a place where the magic happens, and we usually come out with some new revelations because we're combining perspectives and remaining open to the flow of ideas.

Remember, when you introduce a new solution, it will quickly encounter tens, hundreds, or thousands of Outsiders. So, it's best to embrace your team's Outsider early.

Five Points to Consider

The first step in solving your quota problem is to think about solving your problem in a new way. While the temptation is to start with the data and generate numerous analytics, you can easily end up with numerous analytics looking for a purpose. Begin by understanding the story, then leverage analytics to complete the narrative and sharpen your Challenge Question. Then break your Challenge Question into its components to start thinking about a range of approaches using the components. At first, this approach may seem unnatural and unlike what you've done before. But it can lead you to ideas unlike any you've had before. I've been using Sales Design Thinking for years, and it has become second nature to engage in design thinking conversations with clients to pose questions, disaggregate the problem, and think horizontally with them and arrive at ideas together. With practice, you'll be surprised to find that you can do the same. When reflecting on Sales Design Thinking, here are five points to consider:

- Push your team to leverage Sales Design Thinking to come out with a solution that is differentiated for your business and solves the unique components of your challenge.
- Think in terms of questions, starting with a Challenge Question that is granular and descriptive and includes the most important areas to solve.
- Push your divergent thinking by exploring the components of your Challenge Question and combining parallels of how others in your industry, outside your industry, and outside business approach each component.
- Invite the Outsider into your design process to challenge your thinking and test your options.
- Practice the Sales Design Thinking process to make it natural and part of your creative muscle memory.

CHAPTER 3

Understanding the Story and Redefining Your Problem

My daughter called me from college. The urgency in her voice mixed with the road noise in the background told me something was up. She informed me that she had been driving at full speed down I-40 outside of Chapel Hill when her Jeep suddenly seized up, stranding her on the side of the road. As a concerned dad, I immediately put my Boy Scout training to work, calling roadside assistance to get her off the shoulder and to a reputable auto shop in the area. Naturally, the tow truck dropped her at a nearby national auto association-affiliated shop which, after a 10-minute inspection, informed me that the engine had frozen up because of a lack of oil. According to the shop, we needed a new engine. The price tag: $5,000. They would be happy take care of it right away, they said. If we waited, we were welcome to keep my daughter's car on their lot—for $50 a day. Very accommodating. And if we wanted to get a second opinion, we would have to tow it to another shop.

I wasn't about to spend $5,000 for a new engine in a car my daughter drove around college. So, like any dad, after I flipped out, I began my research. At $50 a day, the clock was ticking. All the shops in the area quoted me a price for a new or reconditioned engine because they saw that as the problem. I even found some engines on the Internet that I could order and have a local shop install. That was loaded with risk as I could imagine the finger pointing between the installation shop and the engine supplier when something didn't work out with my order.

After hours of searching engine shop reviews, I came across a stack of positive reviews for one shop in particular. When I called, a guy named Jimmy answered the phone. He had a thick New York accent, which stuck out in North Carolina. I felt like I was back in the boroughs. I told Jimmy what happened and what I was looking for. "Mark," he said, "Tell me the story of the car."

"What?" I replied. Nobody had asked me anything like that in my other calls.

"Tell me about the car. When did you buy it? How does your daughter drive it? Has she had any accidents? What kind of repairs have you had?"

Photo by Mark Donnolo

I talked about where we bought it. I confessed that I thought I had paid too much, but it was a good car. I talked about the repairs. Yes, she did have an accident about a year earlier. That really set me off because our insurance rates went up. We had some engine repairs done after that. All this time, I could hear Jimmy on the other end, in his New York accent. "Hmmmmm. Oooooh. Right, right."

"And then we added oil a month ago in Atlanta," I said. "So I know that the car wasn't out of oil."

"Tell me about that," he asked.

After about 15 minutes of this, I had told Jimmy most of the history of the car. "I tell you what," he said. "Bring it in, and we'll take a look at it." I was already sold.

A day later, the phone rang. It was quiet in my office and Jimmy's voice came blasting through the receiver. "Mark, Mark! Are you sittin' down?"

"Yeah Jimmy."

"You're not gonna believe this. You're gonna owe me. You're gonna write me a great review!"

"What?"

"We opened up the engine . . . and we found an old rag in the oil pan." I didn't understand. Was this a set up? "The guys in the shop . . . when they saw the rag, they fell down and rolled around on the floor laughing!" he said. "We just moved your daughter's car to the side of the shop and closed it up. We're not touching it until we get the insurance claims inspector out here."

We traced the story back to some engine repairs we'd had at another shop. The problem wasn't that my daughter hadn't put oil in the car. The problem was when the other shop worked on the car, they accidentally dropped a rag in the engine and didn't see it. That rag absorbed the oil and starved the engine, which eventually froze up.

Naturally, the other shop was surprised. They were great guys who helped figure out what had happened. After their insurance company completed a thorough investigation, we ended up getting a free engine. My daughter wrote Jimmy a stellar review. Jimmy followed up to make sure she did.

If it hadn't been for Jimmy asking us to tell the story so he could get an understanding of the events and players involved, we would never have discovered the true issue. We might have purchased a new engine and the old engine would have ended up being refurbished or scrapped. The first shop would have been happy to take our $5,000 and walk away. But that wouldn't have solved the actual problem.

The Story Behind the Problem

My experience with Jimmy the mechanic shows the importance of understanding the root of the problem. Jimmy didn't start by addressing the problem of a Jeep that needed a new engine. He started by asking about the story behind the problem. He didn't assume that he knew the solution based on what he'd heard in the first few sentences. He asked questions, the answers to which formed the story; and that story became a dimensional Challenge Question that he could solve.

Jimmy had an effective problem-solving method. Let's look at how we can take Jimmy's intuitive process and apply a little structure to it that you can use for your own business. For illustration, I'll describe a client of ours. Keeping with Jimmy's theme, they are a manufacturer of technology products for the automotive industry. They sell electronic components to major auto manufacturers, and they also sell aftermarket products for existing vehicles. They knew they had a problem, part of which had to do with quota setting. As the analytics would show, there were a number of indicators of sales underperformance that may have been due to how the quotas worked. Their problem statement was:

"We need to fix the quota process because the organization is underperforming."

We will get into some of the analytics as we go, but diving into the numbers too soon or too deeply can pull you into the minutiae too quickly and cause you to lose sight of the story. However, you do want to run a standard set of analytics to use as a reference as you put together the story. Think of yourself as a detective getting the standard panel of tests as you begin your forensics at the crime scene. The analytics alone don't tell the whole story, but they do serve as valuable indicators in the investigation.

When understanding the story, examine not only your quotas but also their related sales effectiveness disciplines. The model we use, the Revenue Roadmap, examines quotas—or any other sales discipline—in the context of the four major competencies of successful sales organizations (Figure 3-1):

- **Insight:** Identifies what's happening in your environment, including Voice of the Customer, Macro Market Environment, Competitor Performance, and Business Performance.
- **Sales Strategy:** Uses that insight to inform the direction for the sales organization. Some major sales strategy disciplines are Products and Services, Segmentation and Targeting, Value Proposition, and overall Approach to Market.
- **Customer Coverage:** Includes Sales Channels, Sales Roles and Structure, Sales Process, and Sales Deployment.
- **Enablement:** Supports all of the upstream strategic and coverage disciplines and includes Incentive Compensation and Quotas, Recruiting and Retention, Training and Development, and Tools and Technology.

Figure 3-1. The Revenue Roadmap

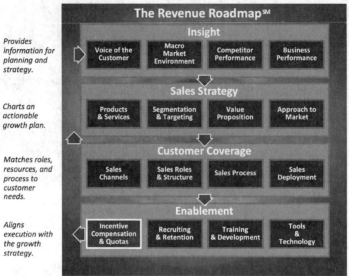

High-performing sales organizations plan, operate, and manage around these four major competency areas and their related disciplines. It's critical to ensure that the quota-setting approach aligns to the related upstream and downstream disciplines, as many quota challenges are actually indicators of misalignments in other sales effectiveness disciplines.

Any of these upstream disciplines can show up in quota setting, which may be the symptom of a larger problem. As you develop your story, ask yourself: *Is it really the quotas, or is it related to other disciplines connected to the quotas?*

Let's take a look at this automotive company in the context of the Revenue Roadmap and its story.

Finding Clues to Understand the Story Behind the Problem Statement

We started with the clues and diagnosis to build the story and identify the dimensions of the problem (Figure 3-2).

What?

We began by getting our client's story behind the problem. We asked questions like, "What happened?" and "What are the pain points?" The organization had been falling short of its quota for the past couple of years. That meant that the company overall was underperforming and too few people were hitting quota to allow the company to hit its goal. We looked at its revenue performance trend over the past several years and saw that it was declining. The company was a historically good performer, but its competition had increased, exposing its sales performance weaknesses.

Figure 3-2. Understanding the Story and Creating the Solution Vision

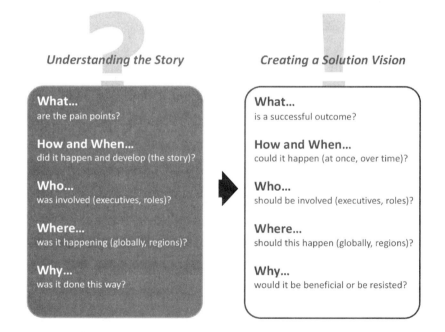

The first analytic we looked at was a distribution of rep quota performance (Figure 3-3). The horizontal axis shows buckets of 10 percent performance increments to quota. The vertical axis shows the number of reps in each of those buckets. What we're looking for is a relatively

smooth bell-shaped performance curve. For this organization, only about 20 percent of the organization was reaching or exceeding quota. Typically, we like to see about 50-70 percent of the organization at or above quota, which shifts the performance curve slightly to the right of 100 percent of quota. There are a couple of reasons for this: First, mathematically having the majority of the organization at or above quota will usually get the company to its goal within the planned sales compensation cost of sales if the design assumed that performance distribution.

Figure 3-3. Distribution of Rep Quota Performance

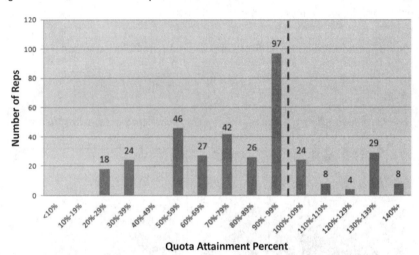

Of course, the company could still get to its goal by having a good number of very high performers and a lot of average performers, but those erratic spikes in performance would probably drive compensation cost out of control if the plan has accelerators for high performance. A smooth, predictable performance distribution is a lot easier to manage than "winning ugly" with erratic performance.

Second, there is a psychological reason for having the majority of the organization at or above quota. Sales organizations operate not only on their planning and analytics but also on their confidence. Think about a sales organization with the majority of people below quota. It's easy to imagine that they probably do not have high self-esteem and might lack the confidence required to win. We want a sales organization of positive people who see themselves as winners. Having a majority of the sales organization at or above quota accomplishes that objective.

We could see that our client's organization had been lagging in performance. Not enough of the team was above quota and too many were below, dragging performance down. At first glance, we might have assumed that the problem was quota setting, sort of like when all the auto repair shops assumed my daughter needed a new engine. Certainly the issue could have been that the quotas were unrealistic, that they didn't represent market opportunity. Poor quota attainment could also be related to performance. There may be underlying issues with the sales roles, sales process, or the organization's discipline to execute the sales process. There could also be an issue with talent; the organization might not have the right people in the right jobs. A poor quota distribution does not necessarily mean that there's a quota problem. With this manufacturing company, quota performance was the top-line issue that was visible to them.

How and When?

Next, we talked with the company about the story. How did it happen and when?

It seems that this issue had unfolded over a period of years. The company was founded several decades ago with a set of core electronics offerings. They grew through acquisition, adding on an antenna manufacturer then a GPS company as well as a few others in automotive electronics. Each acquisition brought a new set of products to the portfolio—and each acquisition brought a new sales organization to be integrated into the company. The degree of integration varied; several of the sales organizations still held on to their legacy heritage, even identifying themselves by their original name with the parent company as a tagline. The result? They had a sales force that was a compilation of several acquired organizations that moved in the same general direction but each with its own areas of expertise and its own preferences about how it did business.

Understanding this part of the story provided a clue: The company had an inconsistent sales organization design and approach to market. Could this be contributing to the quota issues? As we questioned further, we learned that the organization performed well as a whole over a period of years when their products were unique and the market wasn't as competitive. New business was there for the taking, and the sales organization had it good. But as more competition entered the market, selling became a little tougher and the orders didn't flow in as effortlessly as they used to. Leadership questioned whether the sales team had the skills to compete, beyond just taking orders. Concerned about performance, the parent company eventually began to implement more rigorous financial controls. Consequently, goal setting at the corporate level and for each of the acquired companies became more stringent and expectations became greater, which increased pressure on the sales organization.

Looking at *when*, some of the analytics told us what had happened over time. Looking at a multiyear trend of the sales organization, we saw that results were sporadic at the rep level (Figure 3-4). A rep who performed well one year might not have performed well the next year, but likely would have performed well the third year. While we might not know the complete cause of this pattern, sometimes when we see this dolphin-like behavior—reps going up and down year after year—it indicates that there is a quota-setting process based on historical performance. As I described in chapter 1, this type of quota-setting process creates a pattern of overachieving and underachieving.

Figure 3-4. Year-Over-Year Quota Consistency

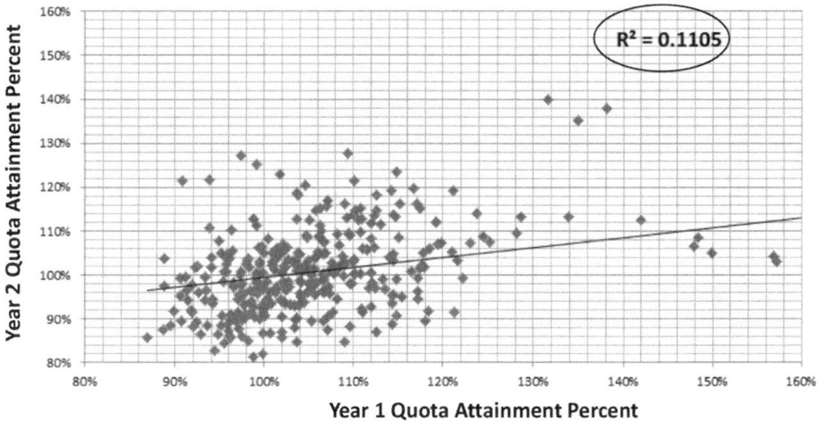

Who?

As the story took shape, we asked questions about who was involved. Of course, senior leadership was at the forefront. Strategically, the acquisitions made sense because the product portfolio from each company appeared to fit well with their target automotive market. As the parent company brought on the new companies, it didn't want to disrupt the flow of business in any of them. The parent company tended to provide a good deal of autonomy to each acquired company. As long as sales teams hit their goals, heads of sales continued to run their teams.

The parent company tried to create some consistency across the sales teams, but the legacy sales cultures were largely unmoved. Some of these cultures were sales oriented, but most were more operations oriented, enamored more by the engineering than the selling. This laissez-faire approach seemed to work well during the heady times. As competition increased and new players entered the scene, the finance organization stepped up and took a stronger role in telling each company how it needed to perform financially.

Where?

The question of *where* has a few important dimensions. Organizations typically don't operate in a homogenous way geographically, by business unit, or by role. "Where" refers to theaters, regions, territories, and offices—the places where things happen. "Where" also refers to where things happen organizationally in terms of business units. When we asked around at our client's company, we learned that each of the markets had different situations in terms of quota attainment. Some markets had suffered significant competition and slower growth, while others had been increasing in potential and growth. As we talked about "where," we learned more about the turnover dilemma; turnover was not high across the entire organization, but only in certain employee groups, one of which was the 75th percentile of performers and above. From their perspective at the top end of the sales organization, their prospects seemed better in other companies. So that group tended to seek new opportunities with competitors.

Another segment of the population feeling the effects of turnover was new hires with less than two years of tenure. With no program to ramp up new hires around quota expectations, the company threw them into the morass of the competitive market before they were ready. New reps did have a draw, which paid them a flat bonus for about a quarter, until they could get up to speed. But the draw program didn't equip them to achieve the goals they would receive following the draw period. As a result, the organization was hemorrhaging, with high turnover of its top performers, high turnover of its new people, a leftover population of middle and low performers, and no source of new talent.

Why?

With some of the story scripted and some of the players identified, we began to look at why these events happened. What were the players' motivations? The lagging financial performance created pressure to get the house in order, and finance was brought in to do it quickly. Senior leadership was motivated to get the company back in line, and finance was the vehicle to make it happen. The parent company had acquired outside funding in the form of debt and equity and needed to make sure that those investors and debt holders were happy. As results turned downward, senior leadership became nervous. The equity holders grew concerned and more engaged in the day-to-day business. The debt holders began asking more questions and looking for more backup reporting behind the business results. Understandably, the finance hammer came down on the sales organization.

Of course, the sales organization wasn't happy. After all, it had grown accustomed to the autonomy that the parent organization granted following the acquisitions. The idea of finance coming in and calling the shots wasn't to their liking. "What does finance know about our customers and sales?" they complained. "We built this organization customer by customer. Finance never carried a bag and it has no idea what it takes to grow a business!" Finance and sales each held its position; each knew it was right. However, since finance had the authority of senior leadership, it ended up imposing some heavy top-down goals.

Quota Qualm: Can Gorillas Teach Us About Myopic Goals?

A Harvard study (Simons and Chabris 1999) humorously highlighted that while goals help us focus our attention, they can also narrow our focus to the point where we overlook what's right in front of us. Participants in the study were asked to watch a video in which two groups of players passed basketballs. One group wore white shirts; the other group wore black shirts. The participants were asked to count how many times the group in white shirts passed the ball to one another. Surprisingly, most participants didn't notice when a person in a black gorilla suit entered into the middle of the scene, pounded their chest, and exited stage right. By concentrating strongly on the players in white, participants overlooked what should have been a conspicuous sight! The gorilla blended right in with the players in the black shirts. I tried this experiment in front of an audience of more than five hundred people and, after the video, only about 10 percent of the crowd recalled seeing the gorilla. This phenomenon reminds us to use quotas to focus the organization, while continuing to emphasize the importance of keeping perspective on new opportunities for growth.

The invisible gorilla (Simons and Chabris 1999). Image provided by Daniel Simons, www.theinvisiblegorilla.com.

Articulating a Solution Vision

After working through the story with this company and turning up all the pain and suffering of the past several years, we took the same set of questions and turned them around to form a vision of what a great solution might look like.

What?

What does a successful outcome look like? In simple terms, it would address all the issues that we identified in our questioning. At a summary level, it would solve the quota attainment problem in a way that will contribute to improvements and company growth. A successful outcome would likely address the inconsistency in sales roles and the sales model. Depending on the organization, the team working on the quota process may have these broader sales effectiveness areas within their control or may need to pull in the people that do have control over those areas. In the case of this organization, the team we were working with did control the overall sales strategy. A successful outcome would also include stemming the sales organization turnover and engaging parties such as finance—to make them comfortable with the predictability of revenue—and sales—to keep them engaged and motivated.

How and When?

With such a potentially significant solution, the questions of how and when are very important. One option may involve introducing the solution in its totality across the entire organization. However, a big change may need to be phased in to ensure that all parties in the organization are engaged and that the solution is tested at each step. This is an important change management consideration. The details should be included in an implementation and communications plan. We'll look at some communications examples in chapter 10.

Who?

In this case, "who" describes the parties, executives, and individuals in the organization that need to be involved for a successful implementation of the solution. Our client could not roll out a solution and mandate universal change. That would have been met with staunch resistance that probably would have made the situation worse. The company knew that it had to get finance's buy-in. They also had to engage sales leadership because that's who would ultimately have to represent the new solution to the sales organization. Getting finance and sales to partner on solution development and implementation would be critical.

Where?

The "where" in our vision involves where the changes will take place. In this case, the change needed to take place across all markets, but most importantly in the markets with the greatest competition. The change also needed to take place across all sales roles, with a concentration on the high performers and the new hires.

Why?

The "why" is critically important because, when you've created your solution, the "why" motivates and drives the big message around change. To make a change, especially a change in the quota process of the magnitude that this organization had to make, there must be a clear message around the reasons for making that change and why that change will benefit each of the parties involved. The "why" had to be very clear to finance, sales management, and frontline sales. When we look at communicating the "why," we consider the audience, the message, and the proof source. For sales management, the "why" would describe the benefit to that group of changing the quota process and areas related to it such as consistency and sales roles. The "why" also needs to look at motivators and timing. For example, the sales organization may be motivated by the benefit of hitting its quotas or the avoidance of additional turnover in the near term. Usually, near-term benefit or avoidance of pain are the strongest motivators.

At last, we take everything we've learned from our initial investigation of the story and development of our vision and put together a concise Challenge Question that redefines the problem statement in more enlightening detail. The Challenge Question summarizes what we're trying to solve for based on the story and key components from our solution vision. I like the idea of using a question rather than a statement because questions promote continued thinking and insight. Open-ended questions tend to provoke more ideas than closed-ended statements.

Let's take a look at the components of a Challenge Question for this company. The Challenge Question is going to be more descriptive than "How do we fix the quota process?" It will start with the elements of the problem that came from understanding the story and vision. Keep in mind, these are only starting points because we will want to investigate further and develop the solution based on our Challenge Question.

A redefined Challenge Question for this company may look something like this:

> *"How can we develop a market opportunity-based quota solution that drives company revenue goal attainment, raises sales organization quota performance with year-to-year consistency, contributes to lower turnover, and responds to an improved sales organization design, while engaging finance and sales as a unified team?"*

As you can see, the Challenge Question incorporates a number of elements of what we learned when we put together the story and came to understand the solution vision, such as:

- company goal under-attainment
- sales organization goal under-attainment
- sporadic year-to-year rep performance
- inconsistent sales model and roles
- sales organization turnover
- quotas that are viewed as an attainable and not based on actual market opportunity
- the need for finance to have predictable performance
- the need to engage the sales organization.

The result of understanding the story and creating the solution vision is a much more specific definition of what we're trying to accomplish and what great looks like, compared to the original problem statement of "We need to fix the quota process because the organization is underperforming." With the story behind the problem told and an initial vision articulated, the Challenge Question provides us with a clear starting point for investigating the problem and building the solution. As you apply your own Challenge Question to the problem, you can further develop it as you learn more. Also, when your team has options for the solution, you can test them against the original Challenge Question and solution vision to ensure that they align. By getting agreement from all parties involved in your organization, the Challenge Question and solution vision become touch points for everyone to ensure that the final solution addresses each aspect of the original problem.

Five Points to Consider

In most organizations, identifying the problem statement around quotas can be difficult in itself because of the intricacies of the issues. To get a more complete foundation for solving the problem, look back to understand the story and then look ahead to create the vision for what a great solution would look like. From that investigation you can define a clear, multifaceted Challenge Question that incorporates an understanding of the problem and a view toward the vision for the ultimate outcome. Pay special attention to the "why" in your solution vision because, once your solution is designed, it may be the "why" that you use to articulate the benefits of the solution and motivate the organization into action. While you're understanding your story and looking ahead, here are five points to consider:

- Don't assume you know what the problem is by looking at the most obvious issue.

- Understand the story of what led to the issue you've observed to build out all of the dimensions and review clues and potential diagnoses beyond your problem statement.
- Create your solution vision for what a great solution would look like and make sure you have a clear statement of why it would be valuable to the organization.
- Articulate your redefined Challenge Question using the key components of your solution vision that describe what's required for success.
- Resist getting lost in the analytics without a plan to use them to understand and solve your problem.

CHAPTER 4

People: The First Dimension of Success

It was a cool evening in April 2017, but the atmosphere was hot and wild. I was crushed in the middle of 50,000 screaming, euphoric fans at the intersection of Franklin Street and Columbia Street in Chapel Hill, North Carolina. After a long season, the University of North Carolina Tar Heels had just won their sixth NCAA basketball championship.

After that event, I thought about the teams that succeed in the NCAA tournament of 64 teams. With more than 350 NCAA Division I men's basketball teams in the United States, why do the same programs show up year after year in the field of 64, the Sweet 16, the Elite 8, the Final Four, and the championship game? That's a powerful Challenge Question. As of this writing, the top-tier teams in terms of championship game appearances are UCLA (12 appearances and 11 championship wins), the University of Kentucky (12 and 8), the University of North Carolina at Chapel Hill (11 and 6), and Duke University (11 and 5). Only 15 teams (the top 4 percent) since 1941 have won more than one championship game. There must be a reason, an approach that leads to success. These top teams don't always have the top talent. Coaches rely on their charisma, vision, and program strength to persuade new recruits. Many players cycle through the top college basketball programs like a revolving door on the way to the NBA. But, year after year, many coaches remain with their loyal rising sophomores, juniors, and seniors plus the next generation of new freshman players.

While the college game continues to evolve, what differentiates the top programs? People, process, and resources. The people side includes coaches who have superlative leadership skills, who can chart a vision, and who can train and develop their players to compete as a team rather than as individuals. The core of the people are the players, many from diverse backgrounds and different perspectives. A lot of players start as lone wolves, individual stars, not yet team players. But they are coachable and, in the end, they share a common vision.

On the process side is a methodology for how to develop the team and how to play the game. I was fortunate to take a tour of Dean Smith Center in Chapel Hill with Scott Smith, the legendary coach's son. What he showed us made the point. In the post-game film room, where the coach and team review video of each game, a stats board hangs to the side of the video screen. On one axis of the board each game of the season is listed. On another axis the key metrics are listed for each game. The list includes metrics such as blocks, assists, screens, and rebounds with the leading players for each metric. There is, however, one metric that isn't included: points scored. The process of winning is based on critical factors to be executed. Follow the process and play like a team. The points will come.

Resources provide the facilities, trainers, and programs that enable a winning team. Of course, some teams have invested heavily up front in making a run at a championship. But with the perennial winners, often a successful coach and a successful process will help with recruiting talent that leads to a winning record that ultimately draws the funding and resources to help the team continue to build into the future. With quota setting, leadership and coaching is paramount. A strong leader with a clear vision and process can draw talent and investment in improving quota competency that will help the business grow. When we look at disciplines like selling, creating winning sales strategies, and developing a game-changing quota approach, the people, the process, and the resources are paramount.

Introducing the Quota Success Model

Conventional wisdom holds that setting effective quotas is all about the numbers. But if that were true, quota setting would be totally analytical, based on fact, and completely objective. If it were about only the numbers, it would be a lot less messy and a lot less emotional. We'd have fewer turf wars about who owns the process, sales and finance would love each other, and there would be little to no emotional turbulence from managers and reps who've been saddled with an unattainable goal that they fear will "bottom out our sales compensation plans" and "destroy our financial futures!"

Sales Design Thinking relies on the principle of simplification. Most of the challenges we deal with in sales problem solving have a good deal of complexity and "hair" on them. Quotas, in particular, are a hairy issue for most companies because they involve market information that may be incomplete, capabilities of the sales organization that are hard to define, people with views that are hard to understand, and the sales organization's compensation, which can become a hot, emotional issue. Let's look at the big, global Challenge Question around quota setting that we address in this book:

> *"How can we develop better methods and processes to improve how organizations set attainable quotas that drive company performance?"*

There are many answers, of course. When we explore "methods," "processes," "attainable quotas," and "company performance" we find three fundamental dimensions that describe the practices of high-

performing sales organizations. Examining these three areas can simplify how we approach the problem:

- the **people** who engage in setting and receiving quotas
- the **market opportunity** that's available to the people in the
  sales organization
- the **sales capacity** of the people in the sales organization to
  pursue that market opportunity and attain those quotas.

We've taken a leap from a very complex challenge to three dimensions that can help us simplify and solve the challenge.

Keep those three dimensions in mind. The Quota Success Model is
built on them (Figure 4-1). The model looks at how organizations go
about planning and exceeding their growth goals in the context of the
roles and process the organization engages to create goals and allocate
quotas (people); what's available and addressable in our markets based
on where we focus and what we offer (market opportunity); and our
ability to win more than our fair share of the market opportunity and
achieve or exceed our goal (sales capacity).

Figure 4-1. The Quota Success Model

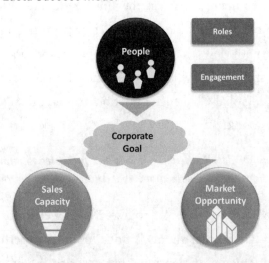

This chapter looks at the people dimension. In the chapters that follow, we'll look at market opportunity and sales capacity. Then we'll look at some methods we can apply to the overall process.

Quota Qualm: Why Couldn't the Optical Manufacturer See This Coming?

Back in 1993, lens division managers at Bausch & Lomb were on the verge of missing their annual sales targets. For years, a soft lens known as SVS—lenses that were worn for around six months—had dominated contact lens sales. But now, SVS was losing market share to disposable lenses. Fearing the cannibalization of its own product lines, Bausch & Lomb was a late arrival in the disposable market. Consequently, the contact lens division found itself playing catch-up against its rivals. With SVS sales flat, sales executives knew they wouldn't make their numbers. But senior management wouldn't budge.

Setting aside caution—and good judgment—sales leaders threatened distributors: either buy two years' worth of inventory at artificially inflated prices or lose their distributorships. These strong-arm sales were booked as revenue even though some of the distributors were told that they could return unsold inventory. This was an SEC rules-of-revenue violation. After the regulators took action, Bausch & Lomb and four of its former executives agreed to settle the charges that they overstated revenue and earnings by improperly booking sales. Plus, the company paid $42 million to settle a shareholder class-action suit. Both its stock and its reputation took a nosedive. Thomas Newkirk, then-associate director of the SEC's enforcement division, summed it up: "If you're going to flog your people to make their numbers, you need to make sure they're not engaging in the kinds of antics that were present here."

Regardless of the perceived upside, never let the wrong expectations overtake the organization.

Enter the Team

While quota setting heats up for most companies around midyear, quotas are at play all year long. Management is (or should be) continuously evaluating the organization's performance, looking at results for each month and quarter, making adjustments to the sales coverage model based on performance, and using that information to plan for the coming year. As the game clock ticks, we see figures in motion. It's a company deep in the midst of operations, moving quickly but purposefully down the court. The team appears:

The Board of Directors

Silhouettes appear high above the court in the owner's box, standing shoulder to shoulder. There are eight of them, maybe 12, with a bird's eye view of the action, gazing at their board books. This sage group is intensely reviewing and approving the big plays, the strategic recommendations of the C-suite executives. The board is focused on the "why"—the vision, performance to the major goals like corporate revenue, bookings, and profit.

In more than a third of companies, the board leads or supports setting the corporate goal versus just reviewing and approving the C-suite recommendation, so the board of directors can be a major player in the process and highly involved in the direction of the business. At most other points in the quota process, the board plays a minimal role or no role. Bill Thomas, former president of Western Union and Bristol Myers-Squibb, discusses the role of the C-suite and the board:

> If you've got the right people in your organization, you can look at the market and the trends, the stock price, and what you need to be doing. Everybody wants the stock price to go up. So, we'd like it to appreciate 5 percent next fiscal year; what does that then translate to in terms of how many dollars this company has to deliver to get that 5 percent growth in the share price? That number, generally, from

my experience, isn't something that the board does. The board would concur that, "Yeah, that's about right, sounds good to me, might be some challenges." But, the board doesn't sit around and come up with that number. That's the job of the CEO or the chief operating officer to present to the board. "Here's what I think the number should be, here's why, and here's how we're going to do it." And then, once it's locked in, the CEO would say, "OK, where are my operating divisions? I'm going to start the process of allocating that number out," and then that starts to cascade down through the entire organization. It's rarely a bottom-up number at this point. A bottom-up number would be next to impossible to really manage in a multinational organization that's spread around the world.

In mid-cap and private equity–owned companies, the board tends to play a more active role beyond just reviewing and approving the goal. In fact, sometimes board members can be overly engaged, as Todd Abbott, executive vice president of global sales for Mitel, describes. "I had a board member who literally was proposing a 20 percent uplift on sales rep goals. And she was saying that's what she has experienced in software. I mean there's no way. I'd have a sales team so demotivated. Now, fortunately, I had a CEO that had the same reaction I did. But, I think there's always this healthy debate."

The CEO, COO, and President

Not far from the board, the executives direct at the top of the organization. Commanding before the board of directors, they look ahead, eyes focused on the scoreboard and game clock, planning for each quarter, the full game, and the rest of the season. From the court below, the entire team looks to the C-suite for strategic direction. The C-suite charts the vision, goals, and strategy for the organization. They also lead the corporate goal-setting process in a majority of organizations. Jana Schmidt, CEO of Harland Clarke, describes her involvement: "I'm accountable for top line and bottom line, establishing how much of that top line is coming from recurring revenue that's already sold and differentiating the recurring revenue from new sales that need to happen and new bookings that need to happen within a given year so they've got time to build. This also helps us to achieve our revenue and margin goals and set a budget."

The CFO and Finance

Walking in long strides back and forth across the owner's box is the CFO, the minister, head held high, focused on the big picture. Behind the CFO streams the finance organization double-stepping to keep pace. The CFO is the watchperson for the C-suite, making sure the team gets a return on its investments in talent and infrastructure. The CFO is also engaged in setting the corporate number in most organizations, along with the CEO, COO, and president. The CFO interfaces with the market analysts to give them insight and temper their expectations. According to Frank Hall, CFO of Radian, the CFO isn't always aligned with the analysts: "They may either have you too high or too low relative to what the business is able to do. So, it always makes me laugh a little bit when the headline says, 'Company exceeds analyst expectations.' The assumption is that the analyst expectation was the right number, versus the company actually producing the right number, and the analyst getting it wrong."

The finance organization comes in close behind, keeping tabs on goal allocation to the organization then leading the top-down, bottom-up reconciliation at the end of the quota-setting process to make sure the organization's number tallies up.

Senior Sales Leadership

At the top of the business units, theaters, and divisions stand the senior sales leaders. They're the field generals. We see them poised on the sideline, looking over the game, charting the plan, directing the players, and making adjustments as the game ensues. The senior sales leaders are assessing the opportunity in the markets, evaluating the sales capacity of the organization, and determining the players and capabilities they need to win each game. They're also allocating the quotas to their division and region sales leaders in the field. Sometimes those quotas are attainable and winnable by the field sales managers. Sometimes the senior sales leaders have to hand down orders that they know are simply too much for the field to handle in the market.

"Our process typically starts with a discussion with the CEO in which we set revenue and profit goals for the upcoming year," said Radian's chief franchise officer, Brien McMahon. "Even if the market expectations are below last year, typically the number will be higher, as we must show growth," he told me. "I receive the number, and then I will typically add revenue to create a stretch goal for our team. So if some people miss it, others will compensate and we'll still hit the original goal that was set."

Marketing

Backing up the sales team, marketing is providing intelligence on the market, the competition, and where we can score points. It often has a big view on the field of customers and competitors, complete with game stats on every angle. Sales leadership has to take this insight and translate it to focused goals, align the right sales capacity and talent, and create game plans for how the team will reach those objectives.

Division and Region Sales Leadership

Suited up on the court, the division and region sales leaders direct the team of field managers and their front line. They're close to the action. They provide bottom-up input to the goals in about half of companies and help allocate the goals to first-line sales managers and the front line. They also swoop in to help their first-line sales managers make adjustments, rally the troops, and win each play.

Sales Operations

This is the group at the core of the team. Behind the results and the accolades that sales receives while it's winning in the spotlight, sales operations supports them across multiple fronts. Sales operations plays a range of mission-critical roles from market planning to account strategy, sales talent development, compensation, and—of course—quota setting. They play a combination of lead and support positions depending on the company and the sales discipline they're covering. Without sales operations, sales would have to scramble to enable its game plan.

When it comes to quota setting, they're often the voice of reason, as Diane Boudreault-Owen, vice president of sales operations for Poly describes:

> I view my role in this process as Switzerland, playing at a very objective level. It's very important that I come in with a neutral perspective, and that I don't show a bias, and I show that I am willing to, and do in fact challenge assumptions of the sales organization, and be an advocate of the organization at large. I need to create a circle of trust, because there is an interpretation that the fox is guarding the hen house. If you want the sales ops team owning it, they have to be Switzerland.

First-Line Sales Management and Frontline Sales

As the intensity of the game continues on the court, we see the first-line sales managers and their frontline sellers engaged in the battle for customers. In the frenzy, it's hard to tell if they're beating the competition and gaining market share or just holding ground. Amid the fray, the managers and reps are in a different reality than those executives up in the owner's box. "We have the business on our backs. Corporate has no clue about what we go through every day. Special projects? Corporate initiatives? The new CRM implementation? What do they think we're doing out here?" they might be saying.

First-line sales management is the defender of the front line. They make sure the front line is trained, equipped, and in winning shape every day. They coach and nurture the front line. They give corporate the stark reality in their bottom-up quota input. But, too often, they feel like the ones in the owner's box pay lip service to bottom-up input and just push down the corporate goal anyway, further distancing the front line from the corner office.

The Game Unfolds—Engagement in the Process

When it comes time to begin the business planning process for next year, we look at the major steps required to allocate that corporate goal to each rep in the organization. The major players get involved in varying degrees, either leading or supporting the process as illustrated from our research.

Determining Market Opportunity

Understand the organization's addressable market in terms of customer revenue retention, customer penetration, and new customer acquisition. Senior sales leadership leads or supports this process in 59 percent of the companies we surveyed, taking the lead 68 percent of the time. Sales operations plays a either a lead or support role in 44 percent of companies, and marketing takes either the lead or support role in 31 percent of companies. Finance supports in 28 percent of companies.

Determining Organization Sales Capacity

Understand what the organization can produce based on factors such as staffing, available sales time, and sales workload. Senior sales leadership leads this process in 63 percent of respondent companies (Figure 4-2). Sales operations primarily plays a support role, engaging more than with the market opportunity determination step, in 59 percent of companies. Division and region sales leadership primarily support in 44 percent of companies. Finance supports 34 percent of the time.

Figure 4-2. Organization Engagement in Business Planning and Quota Setting

Players	Determining Market Opportunity	Determining Organization Sales Capacity	Setting the Corporate Goal	Allocating to Major BUs or Geographies	Allocating to Field Managers	Providing Bottom-Up Goal Input	Reconciling Top-Down with Bottom-Up	Allocating to Reps
Board of Directors			38%					
CEO, COO, President			78%					
CFO			75%	53%				
Finance	28%	34%	63%		25%		54%	
Sr. Sales Leadership	59%	63%	56%	69%	55%	54%	51%	37%
Marketing	31%							
Division, Region Sales Leadership		44%		38%	66%	53%	40%	41%
Sales Operations	44%	59%	40%	44%	62%	56%	50%	65%
First Line Sales Management						34%		59%

Setting the Corporate Goal

Determine the highest-level financial goals to be allocated to the organization. While investor and market expectations weigh into setting the corporate goal, senior leaders in most companies consider market opportunity and sales capacity when finalizing the corporate number. Investors want to increase performance, but they usually want to be realistic and don't want to fall short of goals. A lot of team members get involved in leading or supporting the setting of the big number.

The CEO, COO, or president leads or supports setting the corporate goal in 78 percent of companies we surveyed, taking the lead about 60 percent of the time. The CFO works alongside, either leading or supporting in 75 percent of companies. The CFO's finance organization typically supports in 63 percent of companies, with senior sales leadership close behind, playing primarily a support role in 56 percent of companies. The board of directors either leads (about two thirds of the time) or supports, setting the corporate goal in about 38 percent of companies, otherwise evaluating and approving the goal proposed by the C-suite. Sales operations supports the process in 40 percent of companies.

Allocating to Major Business Units or Geographies

Distribute the corporate goal to the next organization levels, usually business units, regions, or divisions. With the corporate goal set, senior sales leadership allocates the goal to the next level in 69 percent of our respondent companies, leading this about 77 percent of the time. Finance primarily plays a support role with this next level allocation engaging in about 53 percent of companies. Sales operations also supports, participating in 44 percent of companies. Division and region sales leadership plays a support role about 38 percent of the time.

Allocating to Field Managers

Distribute the business unit or geography goals to first-level sales management. Division and region sales leadership conduct this allocation in 66 percent of companies in our survey, usually leading the process and teaming up with sales operations in about 62 percent of companies, usually playing a support role. Senior sales leadership engages in about 55 percent of companies also leading like division and region sales leadership most of the time. Finance plays primarily a support role in 25 percent of companies.

Providing Bottom-Up Input

Use field-level customer and sales information to provide intelligence to the organization as it sets and allocates quotas. During corporate goal setting, allocation to each organization and management level, and allocation to the front line, companies may incorporate bottom-up input. Sales operations is engaged in providing bottom-up input in 56 percent of companies surveyed, balanced between leading and supporting; along with senior sales leadership, division and region sales leadership engaged in just over half of companies, leading and supporting. First-line sales managers provide direct input the bottom-up in about 34 percent of companies.

Reconciling Top-Down With Bottom-Up

Align and reconcile the top-down requirements with bottom-up input in opportunity and capacity. With all the information calculated on the top-down requirements and the bottom-up capability to attain the top-down goal, there's usually a gap or shortfall. For most organizations, this is the final tension point before goals are finalized and locked in for each level of the sales team and the gap has to be reconciled. Someone's got to do it. In 54 percent of respondent companies, finance most often takes a lead role. Along with them, senior sales leadership and sales operations also work on the reconciliation in about half of companies, either co-leading with finance or supporting the process. Division and region sales leadership support in about 40 percent of companies. In our experience, this collaborative engagement is important as goals are finalized to ensure that the sales organization owns the goals. If finance completely owns the reconciliation step then, despite all the hard work the organization does with top-down and bottom-up, the sales team can perceive that, in the end, they were just handed a goal from finance.

Allocating to Reps

Distribute the first-line management goals to the frontline sellers. Sales operations gets involved in about 65 percent of companies in our survey, typically playing a support role to first-line sales management in 59 percent of companies and either leading or supporting, along with division and region sales leadership, in 41 percent of companies. Depending on the company, either the division and region sales leadership or first-line sales management will lead the rep allocation, with the other management level supporting. Senior sales leadership also engages in about 37 percent of companies, usually supporting. In our experience, given an actionable set of tools and development, first-line sales management is usually most effective at frontline rep allocation due to their familiarity with the team and markets. In a solid quota-setting process, first-line sales management's assumptions and decisions are validated by sales operations and sales leadership to minimize any subjective decisions or rep bias.

How Can We Work Together?

With this diverse group of players involved in quota setting, there are bound to be some conflicts and fouls. Everyone comes from a perspective where they believe they're right and they understand how quota setting should be done. With this natural organizational tension around quota setting, here are some practices in organizations that we see are doing it well.

Understand the Motivators for Each Function

The C-suite, finance, sales, and marketing may each have different objectives and motivations during quota setting. For example, finance may be motivated to control costs and get a return on the company's investment in sales resources. That could translate to the voices we hear from finance, which sound like, "The sales organization makes too much for what they produce." Meanwhile, sales may have a different view, which sounds like, "We want the team to beat its quotas, but the organization needs to understand that at the same time, we take our fiduciary role seriously." Marketing may look at the situation from yet another angle, which sounds like, "We have to do everything we can to motivate the sales team to sell our new subscription services, so let's make sure we put enough quota on those."

The key is alignment. Todd Abbott spoke of this. "My experience has always been when finance owns the quota-setting process, it's done from a perspective that is more done from a financial protection perspective versus really aligning to the growth strategy, and the growth plan for the business," he explained. "I think it's important that it's transparent, and everybody understands it, and has signed off on it. But it all starts with 'Do you have a good sound business plan that starts with what's the target addressable market? How big is the market? What's your market share?' If it's not aligned, then setting quota is a little bit of black magic, and, frankly, much tougher to sell to the field."

Create a Common Definition of Success

While each function may have a different perspective, left unchanneled, those differences can put the C-suite, sales, finance, and marketing in continuous friction. Find the commonality in how each function defines success, then work backward from that common definition to understand the differences and how those might be bridged with the process and methodologies the organization applies. It's easier to find commonality when we start from the common point of agreement, then break apart the differences between groups into pieces we can discuss and reconcile one at a time.

Develop a Process With Rules of Engagement

As we'll describe in later chapters, being clear about the process and making it known and visible to the organization creates a path for success. Get quota setting out from behind the closed doors of the conference room. Publish the process. Then define the roles each function will play, the rules of engagement for who will lead and support, and how each function will interface.

Agree to Methodologies for
Each Market Type and Sales Role

Break apart the problem into its components by market type and sales role. Trying to solve the problem by getting each of the functions aligned around a methodology is easier if we develop methodologies specific to the major differences in markets. For example, finance may have greater comfort around trying a pipeline opportunity estimation process for large accounts if the organization is using a more analytical approach such as account potential estimation, which looks at predictors of potential for mid-sized and small accounts that comprise a large portion of the business.

Look to Senior Leadership to Set the Tone of Teamwork

Depending upon the culture of the organization and its level of cooperation, trying to influence and bring along a diverse group of people across functions will only take us so far. Nothing drives alignment like leadership. Senior leadership must make clear the importance of improving quota setting, establish the big "why" behind solving the problem, and demonstrate an expectation of alignment and cooperation for the common goals of the business. When alignment doesn't happen, leadership also has to address it clearly and quickly. If there are active resistors in the organization, leadership must have the resolve to correct them or, if necessary, remove them from the organization. In my experience, when this happens once, the organization suddenly aligns with a great attitude.

Five Points to Consider

People are the first dimension of the Quota Success Model, and ensuring you have clear roles and rules of engagement is critical. With the roles defined, understand the motivators of the team and create a common definition of success. Look back to your solution vision from chapter 3 to pull out the big "why" for improving the quota approach to align the team to the vision. As you think about your team and people, here are five points to consider:

- In quota problem solving, draw upon the three dimensions of the Quota Success Model: people, market opportunity, and sales capacity.
- Lay out the functions and roles that must be involved in quota setting in your organization.
- Align the functions to each step in the quota process and be clear about rules of engagement.
- Create a common definition of success across the functions while understanding their varied perspectives.
- Engage senior leadership to set the tone of the bigger purpose and the importance and expectation of team alignment.

CHAPTER 5

Market Opportunity: The Second Dimension of Success

My family traveled to Iceland over the summer. It's an incredible place—abundant in beautiful scenery and natural wonders. It also gets about 20 hours of sunlight a day in July. We stayed in Reykjavík, across the street from the beach, which was actually a mix of black stones and dark gray sand that flowed into the North Atlantic Ocean. Across the horizon we could see mountains jutting up endlessly. Reykjavík is a bustling city, and at the time Iceland was in the finals of the World Cup, so the city was even busier, bursting at the seams with soccer fans.

We rented a car that could hold our luggage as long as half of it was in our laps. On one of our day trips, we drove several hours and found ourselves in an area called Gullfoss. One of the most beautiful waterfalls I could imagine was powered by a river sourced from a distant glacier that expanded into a series of curved walls of water, complete with its own rainbows formed from the mist above.

It was lush compared to our next stop farther north. We drove through a desolate landscape, totally flat except for boulders and brown dust that extended for miles in every direction. On the side of the road I noticed tire tracks that looked like they were from a lunar lander. In the distance, dormant volcanoes loomed on the horizon. I recalled that part of the movie *Interstellar* was filmed there. We could have been on

Mars. Having come from bustling Reykjavík to this barren place I looked around and, of course, thought about territories and quotas.

What would a sales rep do here? How big of a territory would such a person have in order to carry a quota of any significance? How much harder would it be to carry a bag here than in Reykjavík, where customers are on every corner? These are the things I ponder. This place was a great metaphor for what happens across markets on any continent when we look for sales opportunities, places to go to market with our sales force, and how to plan and set challenging goals. Well, goals here would be challenging. This extraterrestrial landscape illustrated why understanding market opportunity is critical to setting effective goals. For a sales person, understanding market opportunity is also critical to knowing where to find sales in an environment of an unchangeable territory and quota. Most reps have scant information on the size of their addressable markets and are surprised to find hot spots of opportunity they weren't aware of. Like too many companies, if you were to allocate goals like spreading peanut butter, you would end up with huge disparities that didn't account for the real sales opportunities in each market. Spreading peanut butter makes great sandwiches but terrible quotas.

Beyond the Historical

Most of the time when sales leaders set quotas, they're thinking about market opportunity. And many of those leaders think of market opportunity only as historical performance, not future possibilities. They try to project a market's future by looking in the rear-view mirror at what happened last year or over the past several years.

Our research at SalesGlobe shows that 65 percent of companies use some form of historical method when setting quotas, which may highlight one reason it can be so difficult for companies to be forward looking. Correctly estimating future market opportunity is critical to setting challenging-but-achievable sales quotas. In this chapter, we'll look at market opportunity from the perspective of goal allocation as well as a variety of internal and external factors. In the next chapter, we'll look at balancing the sales capacity that will enable your organization to go after that market opportunity.

For many sales organizations, setting quotas is about taking a huge corporate goal and allocating responsibility to the front line in the least painful way possible (Figure 5-1). The head of sales works back and forth on a goal from senior leadership, often the CEO or CFO, that they know is impossible to attain. "The CFO always wants more," says Todd Abbott, executive vice president of sales and marketing for Mitel. "I'm always trying to strike the right balance because the dangerous thing is over-assignment, where you get the disconnect of a CEO standing up every quarter, talking about how great we're doing from plan, but yeah, you've got 50 percent of people making quota."

Figure 5-1. The Quota Allocation Flow

The executive team negotiates the number using whatever information is available on historical capability or opportunity in the market. Marketing provides an abundance of high-level information that cites analyst reports. The head of sales thinks, "Marketing just doesn't know what customer demand really is. It's all broad strokes. Finance has never carried a bag. I'm in front of customers every day and I know what they're going to buy. Taking on this goal is a fool's errand." Sales may get a little leeway from senior leadership, then use it to pad the goal that gets handed down to the next level, just to increase the odds of hitting the number. So begins the quota allocation death march from the big corporate number down to the business units, then to the regions, and eventually to the front line. All the managers and reps get their numbers—usually with little bottom-up input. And most have one thing in common: they don't believe that their quotas are realistic.

Where does it start? The number often comes from on high in the form of a corporate goal. Shareholders want great returns. Yet often their expectations are unfettered by actual opportunity in the market or the capability of the sales organization. Setting the expectations too high and then falling short can drive a public company's stock performance in a negative direction. So it's critical for investors to balance expectations with reality. For private companies, pushing hard on the growth expectation and falling short might not have a detrimental effect; it could even prompt the team to perform. But the sales organization still pays the price in terms of missed goals and lost incentive compensation opportunity.

When it comes to public companies, industry analysts have views, often wide ranging, about the company's expected growth. These expectations may be based on broad sweeping market growth projections applied without understanding the company's capabilities. As Frank Hall, CFO of Radian Group, explained, it's his organization's responsibility to "inform those analysts as best we can," so that they'll set the market's expectations realistically. "I would say of those 15 [analysts], there are half a dozen that I would call true experts on our business and our company. And as long as they're getting the material components of what we're doing, that's the best we can do," he says. "We want to help them produce a high-quality product when they issue their reports on the company, but at the same time, [analysts' reports are] one data point that we'll take into account."

The business has its requirements for growth as well. The C-suite typically has a balanced interest in driving growth and hitting that goal. But, as most of us know, CEOs, COOs, and presidents don't ascend to their roles by holding back but by boldly driving ahead. As I described in the last chapter, the interplay and communications between company leaders can mean the difference between setting a realistic corporate growth expectation and overburdening the organization with an uninformed goal.

Quota Overallocation

From the corporate goal, the number is allocated to the first level, often the theaters (Americas, Europe, Middle East and Africa, and Asia Pacific, for example) or business units. These groups look at the financial aspects of the corporate goal, such as revenue, bookings, units, total contract value, and profit. They also determine which products will contribute to the goal and consider industry verticals to understand what types of customers will comprise the goal. Starting from the top, each level looks at the level below it and decides how to allocate its goal to the next level. Eventually, the region leaders will allocate the goal to their managers or to the frontline reps. According to Tom Farrow, senior director of commission and sales analytics at Charter Communications, "It comes from the top down as to the numbers that we have to hit. The actual quota setting process typically occurs in sales finance, or sales operations," he explained. "Where from the top down, they divvy out what the company has to do, and then sales ops, and sales finance divvies it up based on the regions, territories."

While this happens in an orderly fashion, the manager at each level may add a little tax to the next level down in the form of a few percentage points of additional goal, just in case that next level down doesn't meet its number. Known as overallocation, over-goaling, or uplift, this is a practice most sales organizations use to build in some insurance in case their reports fall short of their quotas, to make up for any open quota-bearing positions that aren't producing revenue at any point during the year, and to cover the ramp-up of new hires who aren't at full quota productivity (Figure 5-2).

Figure 5-2. Percentage of Companies That Overallocate Quotas

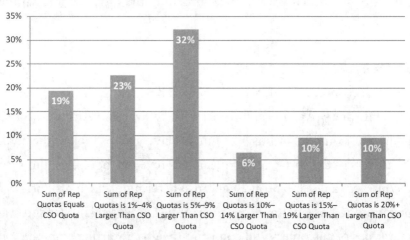

While managers may think that all they're doing is ensuring next year's number, they may be creating two classes within the company: the haves and have-nots. Let's say each management layer adds 5 percent overallocation to the level below it. As the number cascades down three or four levels, the frontline goals could end up at well over 20 percent more than the company goal! "I think there's always this healthy debate on how much to uplift," Todd Abbott told me. "Whether it's three, whether it's five, or if it's a high-growth business, how much you uplift is always a little bit of healthy tension."

The degree of overallocation varies across companies. Organizations with stable, mature, or predictable business models tend to overallocate less than companies in high-growth modes with a large portion of their revenue coming from new revenue and less mature offers that have more variability in results. About 55 percent of companies overallocate the goal from the CSO less than 9 percent by the time it reaches the front line. On average, the practice ranges between 5 percent and 7 percent.

Too much tension and the organization may face two sets of realities: the company reality and the frontline reality. A senior executive from a large transportation company we worked with called me a year ago and posed this dilemma. "We had a great year and the stock was up. We were all remarking, 'Isn't it great? We made our number and had a fantastic year!' But at the same time, we were putting a large number of reps on performance improvement plans for falling short of goal." After I asked a few questions, he disclosed that they had overallocated their quota from the top level to the front line by about 25 percent. While the leaders were celebrating, the frontline reps were thinking, "Gosh, I don't feel like I made my number," and "How am I going to continue in this job if I can't make my number?"

Bottom-Up Input

As the number is cascading down the organization, a second thing should happen: bottom-up input from the field. In organizations that set quotas well, bottom-up input usually happens before the corporate goal. The bottom-up input should inform the corporate goal. This input is not hedging, positioning, or sandbagging by sales managers and reps with the intention of getting a lower goal, although that often turns out to be the case. Think of the bottom-up, top-down process as a "conversation" among the tiers of the sales organization—a dialogue that keeps all parties informed and in which all parties participate periodically throughout the year. Jana Schmidt, CEO of Harland Clarke, described it this way: "I'm setting strategy for the next year, and for the longer term. I'm doing strategic planning, product planning, and sales planning, and bringing those together. You need to get your sales team and your finance team to define what good looks like. For your sales team, it's in their best interest to sandbag out of the gate. And it's in your finance team's best interest to assume they've sandbagged, so they push harder. Then, I can ask, 'does that bottom-up number help me achieve that strategy?' Setting the roles up front is what I try to do. I want you to bring to me what is realistic. So, bottom up, what do you think your territory can do?"

Typically, first-line sales managers provide intelligence to sales leadership about opportunities and buying patterns on a monthly or quarterly basis. That intelligence is used for planning, forecasting, and goal setting. Far from being independent reports, this intelligence should supplement the information that sales leadership and marketing have to sharpen and make their data more complete. As Radian's Frank Hall told me, "The top-down goals are informed by the bottom-up input that we see throughout the year."

During quota setting, when leaders and managers are allocating the number to the next level, the bottom-up input should be considered. In response to that number, field sales managers should provide the latest bottom-up intelligence as quotas are finalized. Managers must ultimately own their quotas and the process of setting quotas at the field level. To test this, I use what I call the pronoun test. When managers talk about "our quota process" (field management) versus "their quota process" (corporate), I have a good indication of whether they are engaged and own the process or see themselves merely as recipients of the number.

If the bottom-up process is left to the end, it's likely there will be large gaps between the top-down requirement and the bottom-up opportunity, and bottom-up input will be used as more of a negotiation technique than a planning approach. Unfortunately, reconciling the two numbers can become contentious, emotional, and painful, leaving the sales organization with an insurmountable top-down biased goal. Charter's Tom Farrow had a few thoughts on bottom up: "There is typically a bottom-up voice, especially after one or two iterations at a minimum," he told me. "So, from the top down, 'This is what it is,' period, end of statement, and then it goes down, so to speak, and then they come back up, and say, 'Well, this is the most we can do, or we can do this.' All salespeople aren't sandbaggers. I've seen a lot of sales leaders that say, 'I can do more than that with the existing population, and we can take more of that load.' So, the bottom does have some influence and persuasion as to what their number is going to be, but it doesn't always make them happy."

By the time the quota is set for the front line, the bottom-up, top-down conversation should have been happening all along the way, leaving managers and reps with a clear understanding of how their quotas were set and why they are what they are. As Todd Abbott put it, "The rationale behind the number is really critical, especially to the field leadership team." If the first-line manager is going to own the plan, says Abbott, he has to be able to say, "Wait a minute, this doesn't make sense." The conversation should never be one way. "I never want it to be, 'Hey, you know, I really don't want your input, thanks,' because then you're just creating the risk that they're not bought in. And I never want that to happen."

Quota Qualm: Does Sales Forgive All Sins?

In May 1968, the Ford Motor Company's then–vice president Lee Iacocca made a brash announcement: The company would introduce a domestically manufactured subcompact that would retail for less that $2,000 and weigh less than 2,000 pounds. The Ford Pinto, he declared, would be designed and developed on an accelerated schedule and made available for purchase in 1970. It was a tall order from Iacocca. Consequently, in the name of speed to market, many in senior management ignored key safety checks during the design and development process. The Pinto's gas tank, it turned out, was dangerously close to the rear axle. In the event of a collision, a Pinto could explode.

Even though Ford discovered this hazard, the company rushed ahead with production, justifying their decision with what in retrospect looks like some pretty creepy math: The cost of paying off lawsuits for accidents involving the 3.2 million Pintos that rolled off the assembly line would be less than the cost of fixing the design flaw. Fixing the flaw would have cost around $137 million, while anticipated lawsuits for death and injury would run just $49.5 million. In 1977, *Mother Jones* magazine reported that Ford knew of the defects and released the car anyway. While the carmaker was never held criminally liable for the 53 deaths and many more injuries that ensued, its reputation was damaged—a stain that marked the company for years. The lesson here is obvious: goals and quotas are all well and good, but we must also consider the greater good. Sometimes that means stepping back, addressing what no one wants to address, and tempering the number with a measure of ethics. Don't let the importance of attaining quota outweigh your organization's values.

The Quota Success Model and Market Opportunity

Let's take an orderly look at the quota-setting process. The Quota Success Model illustrates the important balancing factors in quota setting (Figure 5-3). At the center, you'll see the top-down and bottom-up goal allocation process. The three dimensions of people, market opportunity, and sales capacity determine how effectively we'll allocate that goal to each level and ultimately to the front line. Just allocating the goal down the center will result in goals that aren't market responsive. Adding in market opportunity creates context for the total size of the market and where that market resides by geography and segment. Rounding out with sales capacity ensures that the organization has the ability—from a headcount, time, talent, and workload perspective—to achieve the goal. Let's look at what drives market opportunity.

Figure 5-3. The Quota Success Model

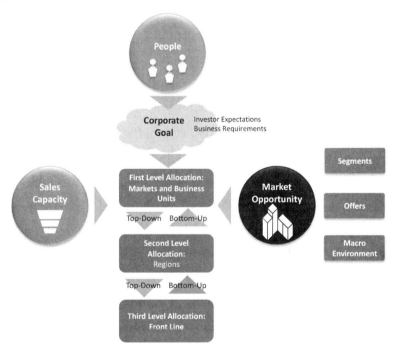

Internal and External Factors for Market Opportunity

To some degree, we can influence the amount of market opportunity available to the organization through internally controllable factors.

Market opportunity can also be influenced by external factors that we can't control.

Internal Factors for Market Opportunity

These are some of the internal factors to consider when assessing market opportunity.

Account Segmentation and Targeting. How you look at certain parts of the market has a lot to do with your TAM (total addressable market), which is the revenue opportunity for a given product or service in any given year that your organization could pursue. Depending on the segments you identify and target, you can increase or decrease the size of your market opportunity.

For example, if you're a manufacturer of dog leashes, you could look at your TAM as one big opportunity. You could sell to any pet supply distributor or retailer that would sell leashes to its customers. Or, you might concentrate on selling your leashes to a particular segment, such as specialty pet retail stores, where your products resonate with customers who have specific tastes. You may then decide to add pet groomers who sell high-end leashes to discerning, fashion-oriented customers. The irony is that as you broaden your market and your sales potential grows, your approach and value proposition may be too general to be effective in all segments in that market. As you define unique segments and understand their needs, your value proposition becomes sharper and better focused, which actually increases your TAM.

You can also increase or decrease your TAM by thinking about size. The same principle of focus increasing effectiveness applies here too. If you target all retailer sizes for your leashes, the market may be large, but it may also be too broadly defined for an effective sales coverage model and value proposition. However, you can apply Pareto analysis—often known as the 80/20 rule—and look at the high end of the market with the largest concentration of potential (the 80 percent) across the smallest number of buyers (the 20 percent), your TAM has become smaller but more concentrated and lucrative. The Pareto Principle, named after economist Vilfredo Pareto, says that 80 percent of the output comes from just 20 percent of the input. In terms of sales, this means that 80 percent of a company's revenue or market potential may come from 20 percent of its customers or prospects (Figure 5-4).

Figure 5-4. Pareto Analysis

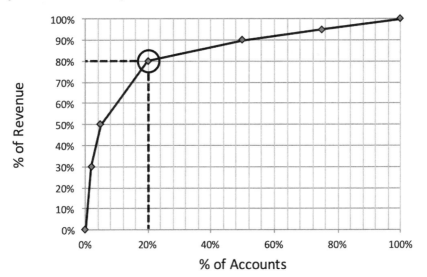

Products and Services. Since the size of the customer base and your portfolio of products for that customer base defines your TAM, what you offer can increase or decrease the size of your addressable market. Offering a single line of products, like leather dog leashes, creates a smaller addressable market than offering related products and services such as fashion leashes (for jogging, casual walking, or evenings on the town), eco-friendly leashes (for the earth dogs), and coordinated collars. The more you expand your portfolio with related products, the more you expand your addressable market, within limits. If your portfolio extends beyond related products—say you add matching ladies' scarves to wear while walking the dog—those unrelated products might not have the market strength of your core portfolio and consequently not align with the same buyers. Buffy may love Fluffy's madras collar and leash as she strolls down Fifth Avenue, but she doesn't want to wear the same pattern around her neck.

Value Proposition. Having a sharper, more focused value proposition can affect your market opportunity. As I described earlier, the better defined your segments, the better you can define your value proposition to each segment and make the opportunity in that segment truly addressable rather than just theoretical. For example, if your value proposition for your dog leashes revolves around "fashion forward," the big-box retailer segment might not see styles and price points they need to attract Buford when he's shopping for motor oil and spots a dayglow orange leash for his trusty bird dog. And unless the actual product or service fulfills the value proposition for the segment (Buford doesn't like madras), that segment won't be in your addressable market.

External Factors for Market Opportunity

These are some of the external factors to consider when assessing market opportunity.

Regulatory and Financial Factors. Changes in financial conditions and regulation can impact the market's appetite for your products or services. This includes monetary policy and shifts (such as exchange or interest rates) and regulatory impacts (such as laws, trade policies, and tariffs). If you're a German-based manufacturer, when the euro is weak relative to the dollar, your pricing for dog leashes and accessories becomes more attractive to American markets, potentially increasing your market opportunity in the United States. However, that euro weakness may also increase your manufacturing costs and lower your margins if you use euros to purchase dog leash components from China while the yuan is strong.

In terms of regulation, shifts in laws or policies can increase or decrease market opportunity. For example, if New Delhi were to pass a law that the millions of roaming dogs in India must be licensed and leashed within the next year, your market opportunity for dog leashes would explode, assuming you have the right product and value proposition for that market.

Technology Innovation. New technology can change the market, what it buys, and how it buys. Say a dog-loving entrepreneur develops a radio-controlled "invisible leash." With this device, dog owners wouldn't need to physically leash their dogs at all; instead a radio transmitter implanted under Fido's skin would enable a state of "leashlessness," where dogs would always walk within three feet of their owners. And say the cost of producing this new technology and installing it in dogs was low enough so that virtually every dog owner could afford it. Sure, some old-school dog walkers would still prefer "hard leashes," but a development like that would surely affect a leash maker's TAM.

Market Expansion or Contraction. Growth rates may be higher or lower in certain sectors or geographies. This includes changes in demand due to national or regional economic expansion or recession and changes in buyer preferences or sentiments (for example, eco-friendly or labor-conscious preferences). The dog leash market may be hot in the Northwestern United States because of the continued expansion of outdoor enthusiast dog owners who demand dog accessories with a low carbon footprint made from reclaimed materials. And Christopher and Jessica like the convenience of buying those accessories when they're picking up their favorite gluten-free craft beer and hummus at their local natural grocery store. That would increase market opportunity among specialty retailers in the Northwest.

Competitors. An increase in the number of competitors or a change in your competitors' capabilities can also affect your market opportunity. For example, all your success with selling dog leashes to Millennials in the Northwest over the past several years has attracted competitor attention and several startups have sprouted with a "buy local" positioning, thus decreasing your market opportunity. Conversely, your position may have allowed you to keep your pricing low and your win rates high, causing competitors to look elsewhere or allowing you to acquire the local competitors, taking out competition and increasing your market opportunity.

Goal Interlock

Up until now, we've been talking about market opportunity in the context of setting and allocating the corporate goal with bottom-up input. There are at least three other perspectives that can come into play, especially for more highly developed, complex organizations. Three simultaneous owners of a company's $1 billion revenue goal could represent these perspectives. Each goal owner wants to do the right thing, and they all have a view on what that is, but they have to operate in a coordinated or interlocked manner (Figure 5-5).

These goal owners are:

Geographies. As mentioned earlier on cascading the goal, that $1 billion corporate goal is allocated across major geographies or global theaters (such as the Americas, EMEA, and Asia Pacific). This may be based on historical performance and indicators of future potential, such as current market share, market growth rates, and the economic environment in each theater. The geographies each own a piece of that $1 billion goal. Unless they have more specific marching orders, they'll sell whatever is easiest, fastest, and best aligned with their sales compensation plans.

Figure 5-5. Goal Interlock

Offerings. The company may have a portfolio of offerings it needs to consider as it allocates that $1 billion goal, and each product owner will own a piece of that goal. For example, a client of ours manufactures network hardware as a main business, but they also sell software and services that complement that hardware. When they allocate their goal, they break it into hardware, software, and services as well as some sub-categories within those services. Product marketing may own these goals, often with separate subowners for each product group. Each group is motivated, usually with its own goal and incentive compensation plan to maximize the sales of its product. One way is by winning over the mindshare of the sales organization and sales channels (such as distributors, resellers, and partners). This may be done by providing sales support and adding extra marketing funds and incentives to the sales organization and its partners.

Industries. The company may also have industry or vertical teams that are responsible for selling into a particular sector (for example, manufacturing, high tech, or telecom). Each of these teams owns a piece of that $1 billion goal. The vertical teams may have their own sales people that sell independently or work as an overlay to the primary sales organization to support them with industry expertise. Unless otherwise directed, they'll sell down the path of least resistance in their verticals to offer the products their vertical demands in the geographies that demand it to attain their goals in the way that's most lucrative with their incentive compensation plan.

You can see, with three groups—geography, offering, and industry—owning the same $1 billion goal, the company could be headed for a train wreck of confusion and missed expectations. For this network hardware company, left undefined, their U.K. geographic team will make its own assumptions about what products it will sell and what industries to focus on. The services marketing team will have its goals and assumptions about how much service revenue the organization will sell into the United Kingdom and certain industries. Meanwhile the U.K. team has no idea what the services team expects, or it will just dismiss the numbers simply as "marketing projections."

The telecom industry team has its assumptions about selling a certain amount of hardware, software, and services into the U.K. market in a few major telecom and wireless carriers. But the U.K. team has no idea what the telecom vertical team has for its goal and looks at the team members as just "overlay industry guys who can help out if we have a telecom opportunity we can't handle." And the services team has no idea that the telecom team is planning on selling mostly hardware and software because the telecom team members think that an outside partner would better handle services. The confusion begins as soon as the goal setting is finished. And by the end of Q1, the teams are working in silos, underperforming their goals, and looking for someone to blame.

Putting these pieces together during quota setting is foundational to exceeding goals in a coordinated fashion. This practice of "goal interlock" is often overlooked. Each one of these teams has its own expectations, and each has its own goal. But often, their common expectations are not *interlocking*. If you're responsible for quota setting in a multidimensional organization, consider adding the role of "goal interlocker" to sales operations or finance. Pulled from each geographic, offering, and vertical group, the goal interlock team can better set expectations, drive communications, and keep the engines running at the right speed throughout the year as the results come in.

Measures for Quotas

Quotas are set for specific financial measures that are most important for the sales job. Almost always, the performance measures for quotas are defined by the sales compensation plan. These measures include:

Revenue. Some options for revenue are total revenue, retained revenue from current customers, penetrated or additional revenue from current customers, and revenue from new customers. Revenue is the most common performance measure for goals and compensation across companies.

Bookings. This is defined as the dollar amount of revenue that is booked but not necessarily billed when a sale is made. For some companies, a sale is booked and revenue is received simultaneously or shortly after the booking. For companies that sell large deals, services, or projects, a sale may be booked and then revenue received months or years later. For example, a company that sells a large three-year software contract may book the sale but receive or recognize the revenue over the course of the next three years. So bookings become an indicator of the sale, and the company must decide how it recognizes the booking and the revenue in its goal setting, performance tracking, and compensation programs.

Total Contract Value. Often called TCV, this is similar to bookings in that it recognizes the total value of the contract at the time of the sale, even though the revenue may follow later. Total contract value is useful as a measure to recognize major deals up front that extend beyond a year. It's most accurate when contracts are binding and revenue promised in the contract is assured.

Annual Contract Value. ACV is a shorter-term view on TCV. It's often used for deals that have shorter-term contracts or contracts that aren't iron clad and could be discontinued by the customer. By measuring ACV, the company can plan, manage, and pay ahead of revenue while limiting its view and risk to an annual period.

Product Units or Volume. In environments where revenue may fluctuate due to outside factors such as commodities prices, units or volume provide a constant measure. For example, a client of ours sells petroleum products to transportation companies. With the daily fluctuations in the price of crude oil, a rep's revenue can fluctuate based on market prices rather than an increase in sales. So to normalize price and revenue fluctuations, the company bases goals and measures performance on gallons, not dollars.

Contract Renewals. This metric is important for companies with a sizeable recurring base of contracted revenue that depend on renewing those contracts. Contract renewals can be a component of revenue, if measured as contract dollars or percent of contract dollars renewed.

New Deals Signed or Won. "New deals" is a unit metric that looks at the number of deals rather than their dollar amount. In that way, it's a simple measure that's easy to set goals for and easy to pay for. This metric can be modified by setting a threshold for deal size to qualify. For example, a rep may have an annual goal of signing ten new deals greater than $100,000.

Gross Profit Dollars. This is a financial metric that tracks operating profit in dollars. Gross profit dollars are defined as revenue minus cost of goods sold. It's a simple metric as long as the definition is simple and the tracking is clear and trusted by the organization. Gross profit is the most commonly used profit measure for sales goals and compensation because the sales organization typically controls it.

Gross Profit Percent. This is a financial metric that tracks gross profit as a percentage of revenue. Gross profit percent is defined as gross profit dollars divided by revenue dollars. It's a seemingly simple measure but can create profit dollar slippage. If gross profit percentage is measured alone, the sales team may be motivated to pass on deals that are a lower gross profit percentage than the target, resulting in a reduction in revenue. If revenue is connected to gross profit percentage, each incremental revenue and profit is valuable to the rep.

Operating Profit Dollars. This is a financial metric that tracks operating profit in dollars. Operating profit dollars are defined as gross profit minus operating expenses (which are often defined differently by company). This metric is often used for operations and production teams but rarely for sales organizations, which don't usually control operating expenses.

Operating Profit Percentage. This is a financial metric that tracks operating profit as a percentage of revenue. Operating profit percentage is defined as operating profit dollars divided by revenue dollars. It's not often used for the sales organization, which doesn't usually control operating expenses, but is often used for operations and production teams.

Net Profit Dollars. This is a financial metric that tracks net profit in dollars. Net profit dollars are the bottom-line profit of the business.

Most often, it's used for executive teams and as a broad company measure but typically not for the sales organization, which doesn't usually control net profit.

Net Profit Percentage. This is a financial metric that tracks net profit as a percentage of revenue. Net profit percentage is the bottom-line profit of the business. It's not often used for the sales organization, which doesn't usually control net profit, but is used for executive teams and as a broad company measure.

Here's a look at the percentage of companies that use these measures for quotas at the rep level (Table 5-1).

Table 5-1. Frequency of Measures Used by Companies

Measure	Percentage of Companies That Use This Measure at the Rep Level
Revenue	
Total Revenue	45%
New Customer Revenue	24%
Customer Revenue Retention	15%
Contract Renewals	9%
Bookings	
New Customer Bookings	33%
Bookings	27%
Total Contract Value	21%
Annual Contract Value	12%
Volume	
Product Units or Volume	15%
New Deals Signed or Won	9%
Profit	
Gross Profit Dollars	18%
Gross Profit Percentage	12%

Timing of Revenue Recognition

While we can look at the goal from the perspective of what we can sell during the fiscal year, we must also recognize that it may be attained in under a year or over an extended period of time.

The meaning of revenue for many companies is evolving as they shift from traditional premises or product-based revenue to subscription or software-as-a-service (SaaS) revenue.

Traditionally, a software manufacturer would sell a set of several thousand licenses to a customer for a one-time price (often in the millions of dollars), install it at the customer's offices, and charge for implementation and annual maintenance on top of that. A multimillion-dollar enterprise software sale was a big payday for the company and for the reps who sold it. One sale could make a rep's year. The goal was simple and the attainment of that goal and the associated compensation were simple to track. As technology has evolved (think CRM tools, databases, and advanced operating systems), companies have come up with new ways to offer it, which affects how they set goals, manage the business, and compensate the organization.

As bandwidth has developed, those enterprise software systems moved from on-premises (at the customer's location) to the cloud (online). One advantage to the customer is the ease of installing new versions and upgrading the software. Everyone in the customer organization can be up to date and networked across the globe. The software world has changed. The advantage to the software provider is a smoother, more predictable revenue stream. Unfortunately, this also means that those big, multimillion-dollar sales are also disappearing. This leads us to a dilemma in planning, quotas, and compensation. A rep who once would have booked and received credit for a major deal when it was sold now sells a subscription with revenue that trickles in over the period of the contract. The big revenue hit and the big compensation have been replaced by a big bookings win with a future revenue stream.

The subscription service model is not limited to the software industry and has spawned new revenue models in other industries as far reaching as HVAC, where companies that provide systems to large corporations and real estate developers are converting those capital purchases over to subscriptions where the HVAC company will pay for, install, and maintain the HVAC system as a subscription.

For quota setting, the question becomes: How do we set goals and keep the sales organization motivated in a SaaS world? Like a sales rep making the shift from a New York City territory to a desolate region in Iceland, companies with these models are shifting to adapt to a whole new landscape, new metrics, and new expectations.

Five Points to Consider

Market opportunity, the second dimension of the Quota Success Model, defines the total addressable market for the company and the sales organization. Without it, companies fall back on using history or apply assumptions on average productivity per rep. Consider the flow of goals from the top-down corporate expectation to the bottom-up input from the field and how market opportunity can better inform the process. We'll look at several methods that leverage market opportunity in chapters 7, 8, and 9. As you're looking at your opportunities, here are five points to consider:

- Understand the inputs for the top-level goal and how you can best engage in or inform setting that objective.
- Evaluate your top-down and bottom-up process to determine the best flow and interactions for your organization's sales model, complexity, and culture.

- Determine the factors that affect your organization's market opportunity and use those to provide insight for planning.
- Keep quota overallocation to the field within a range that is attainable for the organization and right for the predictability of your business.
- Select measures for your quotas, in coordination with your sales compensation plan design, that best represent successful performance for each sales role.

CHAPTER 6

Sales Capacity: The Third Dimension of Success

It was the big fish eating the little fish, and the even bigger fish eating the big fish. We, the client project team, were in Europe working with a manufacturing company. It was late in the United States but early morning in France; we really had no idea what time it was. Our consulting team had been crunching quota numbers and looking at territory scenarios most of the night following an all-day meeting. At that meeting, the theater managers from the Americas, Europe, the Middle East and Africa, and Asia Pacific had reviewed and questioned the bottom-up quota estimates from the geographic managers in each theater. We facilitated the sessions and provided guidance and data while the theater managers proceeded to tear apart the geographic managers piece by piece.

After each geographic manager's presentation, if the bottom-up plan came up short of the theater manager's top-down goal (and all of them did), the interrogation would begin. The theater managers picked through every rep and every assumption in the plan, looking for the whys that explained the plans and the hows of fixing the plan to meet the goal. The activity was so frenetic that by the end of the day, the conference room had the aroma of a high school locker room.

Still exhausted on day two, we got off the elevator and entered the conference room. Immediately, I saw why the theater managers so ruthlessly berated their direct reports the day before. It was the final round of top-down bottom-up quota reconciliation with the global chief sales officer. Here, theater managers had to present and defend their case for the goal that they and their geographic manager reports would sign up for. Dietmar, the global chief sales officer, arrived loaded for bear.

Each session began with the theater manager presenting a plan. Dietmar would listen politely for five minutes. At minute six, with German precision, he would start in on the manager. He had clearly prepared for each session and knew the information about each market. His approach may have been a technique to get in a few punches early and throw off the manager to expose some vulnerability in the plan where he could find additional quota opportunity. After all, he knew that he would have to take the plan to *his* boss.

Or, it may have been that Dietmar just wasn't a happy person.

Once the niceties were over and the rumble had reached a certain level of intensity, it was clear that Dietmar was going to get his number. It was just a matter of how. But after so much darkness, I sensed some light in the process. Rather than a "cram down" of the goal that would result in each manager accepting an impossible number under pressure, it appeared that the theater managers knew how to play the game. Session after session, when Dietmar went for the pressure point, each manager would break into a bargaining role about what it would take to get the goal Dietmar wanted.

The bargaining was about sales capacity—the people and resources it would take to get the goal.

At the end of the sessions, Dietmar had the number he wanted—and a bill for the cost of resources to get that number. The theater managers walked away with a shopping list of whom they could hire and the funds they could use to get to their quotas.

That evening, after the hostilities, we joined the full team for dinner at a classic country-style French restaurant where we all enjoyed a fine meal, told stories, and interacted like great friends. "Wow," I thought. "It takes a special culture and a strong constitution to set quotas that way. If that's how they work together, imagine what they're going to do to their competitors!"

Though not every organization has the big-fish-eats-little-fish culture—or the fortitude of someone like Dietmar—to set quotas in quite that manner, this one succeeded by taking a deep (and rattling) dive into what its sales force was capable of contributing. Sales capacity is the often-overlooked key to setting effective quotas and building the sales organization's productivity. The tools in this chapter can give you levers to pull that can drive productivity and increase your organization's ability to reach its goals.

Figure 6-1. The Relationship Between Sales Capacity and Market Opportunity

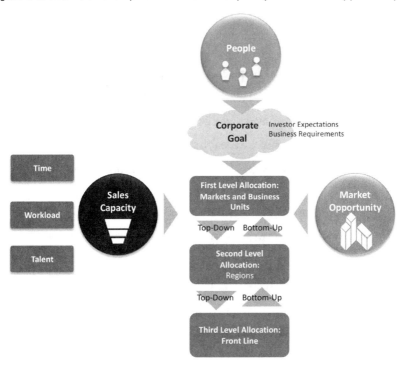

It's important to understand that sales capacity provides access to market opportunity (Figure 6-1). If you look only at market opportunity but not at sales capacity, you're only seeing half the equation. Although setting quotas with market opportunity alone is better than just looking at history, it can leave us without an understanding of whether or not the organization can win more than its fair share of the market—and if so, how? Sales capacity changes the conversation from "Our team can't reach these quotas" to "Here's how our team can reach these quotas."

The Three Parts of Your Organization's Growth Goal

At its essence, sales capacity is the ability of the sales organization to create revenue and attain its goals. This revenue can come through three sources: customer revenue retention, customer revenue penetration, and new customer revenue acquisition.

Customer revenue retention simply means protecting our current customer revenue. Because it's impossible to retain more than we currently have, customer revenue retention from year one to year two can reach a maximum of 100 percent. Sounds pretty basic, right? But keep in mind that the average company retains about 82 percent of its current customer revenue each year (Figure 6-2). So, to grow by 15 percent, a company with 18 percent churn must grow by about 40 percent to make up for that churn! It might not be the glamorous side of selling, but retaining revenue is playing good defense, and it can win the game for your organization.

Customer revenue penetration involves selling more to current or new buyers in the account or selling additional products to the same buyers in the account. Buyer penetration (selling more to current buyers in the account) can come from customers increasing their use of products they purchase from us; or it can come from an increased number of buying points, such as new users in new locations of our customer. For example, if we sell our products to the headquarters location of a customer, buyer penetration could come from users at the headquarters location increasing their usage or it could come from the company using our products at additional branch locations.

Product penetration, or selling additional products to the same buyers in the account, can come from selling extensions or add-ons of our products to those buyers. It can also come from selling new product lines to those buyers. For example, if the buyers at the headquarters location of our customer purchase licenses to our supply chain management system, product penetration could come from them purchasing our account system, which complements it.

New customer revenue acquisition is winning customers with whom we haven't done business before. New customer revenue can come from displacing a competitor or from selling a new customer something they haven't purchased before. Say we're working with a new customer to convert to our supply chain management system from a competitor, or we're getting a foothold with a new customer by taking a piece of what they already purchase from a competitor, such as the accounting system. It's a first step toward winning more business. We could be addressing a need that hasn't been addressed before, either customer-by-customer or in a new market. For example, we might find a company that manages its supply chain through manual methods and spreadsheets and win a contract to install our supply-chain management system. Alternatively, we might find an industry that hasn't commonly used supply chain systems, create a strong value proposition for that industry, and begin selling our products to that new industry.

Figure 6-2. Breakdown of Customer Revenue Retention, Penetration, and New Customer Acquisition

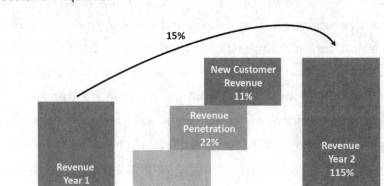

Analyzing Your Sales Capacity

The first step with sales capacity is to break down the organization's growth goal into those three pieces. If your organization has a revenue goal of, say, $500 thousand, identify what portion of that goal will come from retention, penetration, and new customer revenue. As a starting point, take a look at how the organization has grown historically, then determine what you might change to improve retention, penetration, and new customer performance. Here's an example:

Start with line-item data on each account your organization has sold to in the past twelve months. Include each account's revenue at the end of year one and its revenue at the end of year two. Let's look at a simple example of a set of accounts.

First, look at each account and determine what percentage of revenue it has retained from year one. Anything above 100 percent is penetration revenue. For example, if Acme Services purchased $100 in year one and

$85 in year two, we would have $85 or 85 percent retention and $15 or 15 percent churn (Table 6-1). Tally all the retained revenue from all your accounts and divide that number by year one total revenue. This is your revenue retention rate. It's nearly impossible to retain 100 percent of revenue year over year. Therefore, to grow, you'll have to recover revenue that's been churned, either by penetrating current customers or winning new customers.

Table 6-1. Conducting RPN Analysis

Account	Year 1 Revenue	Year 2 Revenue	Revenue Retention	Revenue Retention Rate	Revenue Penetration	Revenue Penetration Rate	New Customer Revenue	New Customer Revenue Rate	Total Growth
Acme Services	$100	$85	$85	85%	$0	0%	$0	0%	-15%
Advanced Tech	$100	$115	$100	100%	$15	15%	$0	0%	15%
Allied Manufacturing	$0	$40	$0	0%	$0	0%	$40	100%	100%
American Central	$140	$70	$70	50%	$0	0%	$0	0%	-50%
Andover Holdings	$0	$12	$0	0%	$0	0%	$10	100%	100%
Applied Software	$120	$206	$120	100%	$85	71%	$0	0%	71%
Total	$460	$527	$375	82%	$100	22%	$50	11%	15%

As Harland Clarke's Jana Schmidt explains, protecting the base is critical to growth. "This balancing to me is very, very complicated and very difficult. And the implications on either side are serious. And I have a philosophy that I share with my team probably every day— certainly every year at this time—if you want to grow, don't shrink the base."

Next, identify your penetration revenue. Calculate the revenue in year two that was greater than the revenue you had in year one. For example, if Advanced Tech purchased $100 in year one and $115 in year two, we would have $100 or 100 percent retention and $15 or 15 percent penetration revenue. Add all the penetration revenue for all of your accounts and divide that number by year one total revenue to get your penetration rate.

Finally, take any accounts at the end of year two that had no revenue with your organization in year one. The total revenue for those accounts is your new customer revenue. For example, if Allied Manufacturing purchased nothing in year one and hadn't been a customer previously, and then purchased $40 in year two, we would have $40 or 100 percent new customer revenue. Add all the new customer revenue for all accounts and divide by year one total revenue to get your new customer revenue rate.

Now you'll have three numbers: customer revenue retention rate, customer revenue penetration rate, and new customer revenue rate. These three percentages will give you a baseline of your current performance. They'll also highlight areas where you might make changes in sales capacity to improve performance. We'll talk about some of those sales capacity improvement areas (such as time, workload, and talent) later in this chapter. We call this analysis RPN for retention, penetration, new. Once you run RPN analysis for your organization, you can get extra actionable insight by running it for each of your territories to see how retention, penetration, and new customer performance varies by rep. You may be amazed at what you see that hasn't been visible to you before. It's like shining a spotlight on sales performance.

Understanding the Sales Capacity Equation

Our clients often ask us to help them determine the sales capacity of their sales organizations and identify areas where they can improve performance. Some have tried it before, using a variety of metrics that provided no answers. For others, it's a mystical question. We'll take the mystery out of sales capacity with simple calculation of sales time and workload:

- **sales time:** the number of annual hours a rep spends on selling

- **workload:** the number of hours it takes a rep to win a new sale (for a new account or new deal sellers) or the number of hours it takes annually to manage an account (for account managers).

The basic calculation for sales capacity is the amount of sales time the rep has per year divided by the workload to win a new sale or new account, which equals the number of new sales or accounts a rep can win per year. Multiply that number by the average revenue per sale or account and that equals annual sales capacity for one rep in a particular role, like account manager (Figure 6-3).

Figure 6-3. Calculating Sales Capacity

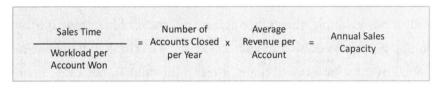

Multiply that total by the number of reps you have in that role and it tells you the sales capacity for that role. Sounds pretty simple, right? Well, let's apply some more detail to it and use a real-world example.

For a financial services organization we work with, an average rep has 2,000 total work hours per year if she works forty hours a week for 50 weeks a year plus two weeks of vacation. (If you're reading this in Europe, you can already see that you've lost an additional two weeks of sales capacity with those month-long vacations.) You may be looking at this and saying, "Nobody works only 40 hours a week. Our people work at least 50 hours a week." You're already starting to pull your sales capacity levers. Apply to that 2,000 hours the fact that reps in this organization spend only 50 percent of their time actually selling because they have hours of nonselling time they spend on activities outside of their core sales roles. It sounds unbelievable; we'll dive into sales time allocation later. So, that leaves our rep with only 1,000 hours a year of sales time.

Next, let's look at sales workload. In our example, this rep is in a new customer selling role. I know a lot of organizations refer to new customer sellers as "hunters" and current account managers as "farmers." A few years ago, we realized that this was just too binary given the multitude of sales roles and the unique DNA required for each role. So, we use what we call our K-9 model, which ranges from dobermans (new customer sellers) to retrievers (current account managers), to collies (customer retention roles) and beyond.

In our example, this doberman spends most of her sales time pursuing opportunities to win new accounts. We'll look at her workload as the average number of hours it takes someone in her role to win a new sale in a new account. Workload isn't just the number of hours it takes to win one sale. It's the number of hours it takes to work through all of the prospects in the sales funnel that result in one closed sale. A rep in this role takes about 63 hours to win a new sale on average. Dividing the one thousand hours of sales time this rep has by the 63 hours it takes to win a new sale tells us that she can close about sixteen sales a year. The average revenue per sale for this doberman role is about $250 thousand. By multiplying the 16 sales per year by $250 thousand of revenue per sale, we can see that the average sales capacity for this role is about $4 million. Multiply that by the 125 reps in this role and we have about $500 million in sales capacity (Figure 6-4).

Figure 6-4. Calculating Annual Sales Capacity

Sales Time / Workload per Account Won	= Number of Accounts Closed per Year	× Average Revenue per Account	= Annual Sales Capacity
1,000 hrs. (2,000 hrs. × 50% Sales Time) / 63 hrs.	= Accounts Closed per Year 16	× $250,000	= $4,000,000 per Rep

How can you increase sales capacity looking at the components above?	1. **Time.** Decontaminate roles to increase sales time allocation. 2. **Workload.** Decrease workload per account through pipeline management. 3. **Talent.** Inventory, develop, and upgrade your team to increase revenue per sale.

You've taken the first step toward getting visibility on your sales capacity relative to your goal. Now, if you are saying, "Well that's not going to get us to our goal," you're in good company because that's the case with many sales organizations.

Quota Qualm: Can Quotas Drive a Conflict of Interest?

Back in the late 1990s, in an effort to hit a number, Sears, Roebuck & Company set sales goals for its auto repair staff of $147 per hour. This unrealistic quota encouraged staff at automotive centers across the country to overcharge for maintenance and repairs and to perform unnecessary work, according to charges made by the California Department of Consumer Affairs. Ultimately, Sears's chairman, Edward Brennan, acknowledged that the $147 per hour quota had motivated the staff to deceive customers. The retail giant's "goal setting process . . . created an environment where mistakes did occur," Brennan admitted. He also announced that Sears was terminating commissions for automotive service employees and ending its controversial sales quotas to help restore consumer confidence. The charges followed an 18-month investigation in which Sears allegedly charged undercover agents an average of $223 for unneeded repairs.

Bottom line for boards and C-suite management: If you can't look stakeholders, employees, regulators, and even customers in the eye and tell them where "the number" came from, you may want to rethink "the number." Define what success means for each job, whether sales or nonsales, and ensure it creates the right customer experience.

The Three Levers of Sales Capacity

Once you understand your organization's drivers of sales capacity, you can determine how you can change each driver and the impact it will create on your organization's ability to pursue market opportunity. Three main drivers are time, talent, and workload.

Bill Thomas of Western Union and Bristol-Myers Squibb describes the importance of aligning sales capacity with market opportunity and quota:

> We did some research on our products—what was driving our products. Let's say we had a sales force of 100 people. Eighty people were directed into doctors' offices to sell our products. They were the demand drivers for the doctors. Twenty percent were sent into hospitals to develop contracts with hospitals to offer our services. When we did research among mothers on baby formula use, we found exactly the opposite. Eighty percent of the mothers said, "I use this brand because it was used in the hospital." Twenty percent said, "I use it because the doctor recommended it." So, our sales resource was completely flip-flopped. I had to change the entire structure of the sales force, so we were putting our efforts into hospitals and not as much in the doctors' offices. So, that required a huge restructuring. I could have passed on it, and said, "No, I really don't want to take that on." But, I always tested myself, I said, "What's the right business decision? OK, let's make this happen." My superiors in the United States were very nervous about this, but they couldn't argue with the research. And we did it, we didn't skip a beat. That's an example of, you've got a sales

quota, but your resources to deliver the quota are not allocated in the right places.

Now let's look at the levers you can pull to increase sales capacity.

Sales Capacity Lever #1: Time

It's 10 a.m. Do you know what your sales organization is doing? Time is one of the sales organization's biggest assets. If a sale rep has phenomenal skills and methodology, they're for naught without the time to sell. Time sounds fundamental, but it may be one of your organization's biggest sales capacity improvement opportunities. Most sales people spend 48-50 percent of their time selling, which means about half their time is spent doing something other than selling. Before these sales organizations even look at any other drivers of sales capacity, they need to recognize that only half their cylinders are firing.

By analyzing and understanding your sales organization's time, rep by rep, your company can "decontaminate" each sales job and increase sales capacity. It's like increasing headcount without hiring. Effective sales organizations decontaminate their sales roles by identifying nonselling activities and eliminating them or shifting them to more cost-effective resources such as sales support, operations, or customer service. These nonselling roles could also be eliminated or decontaminated by using technology or automation more effectively.

The financial services client I referred to has about $500 million of annual revenue in one of its organizations with about 125 quota-bearing reps. Those reps spend only 50 percent of their time selling because they're also handling operational, customer service, and administrative tasks. Why do they do this? Sellers are usually customer oriented and lean toward doing whatever it takes to serve the customer. Calls come in about service issues, operational challenges, or basic requests and often the rep takes the call and attempts to fix the issue. It's the right thing to do for the organization but not for the job. The lines between "sales" and "service" become blurred and, over time, reps find themselves spending substantial amounts of time dealing with these activities that are on the periphery of selling.

Some reps become comfortable with doing these things. "It's my job to serve the customer. I do whatever it takes," they say. These NRGs (non-revenue-generating activities) soon become the norm, and they become a shield of protection from having to improve performance. "Take on more quota? Go out and win more new accounts? I've got too much on my plate with the customers I have." Our dobermans have settled into retriever roles and, over time, have lost their instinct to pursue new customers. The true dobermans usually react differently to the NRGs in their roles. They see them for what they are: job contaminants. They're the first to raise their hands and try to eliminate those activities from their roles. "I'll take on more quota and I'll make more money if I can give these tasks to someone else. Can I get a sales assistant?"

So the reps in this financial services organization spend only 50 percent of their time selling, which, as I described under the sales capacity calculation, totals about 1,000 hours of sales time per rep per year, shown in the first two columns of the Job Decontamination chart (Table 6-2). The $4 million of annual sales capacity per rep is shown in the second column from the right. So, what's the impact of decontaminating the role and increasing sales time? From the example in the shaded row, if we move up just five percentage points of sales time, increasing from 50 percent to 55 percent, that would increase annual sales time per rep from 1,000 hours to 1,100 hours. With that extra 100 hours of annual sales time, let's assume that we don't get the same amount of productivity as we do with the current 1,000 hours because the rep has to determine how to best use that time and maximize their productivity. So let's assume that we only get 30 percent of the productivity per sales hour with those additional 100 hours. That would produce an additional $120,000 of revenue per rep on top of the current $4 million for a total of $4.12 million. Multiply that incremental $120,000 by the 120 reps on the team and that produces incremental revenue for the organization of $15 million. That's quite an ROI for just eliminating nonsales activities or shifting them to other roles.

Table 6-2. Job Decontamination Chart

Job Decontamination ROI

If the Organization Increases Its Sales Time Percent to:	Each Rep Would Have This Many Hours of Sales Time:	Incremental Revenue per Rep Assuming 30% of Current Revenue Productivity Would Be:	Total Revenue per Rep Would Be:	Which Would Have This Incremental Revenue Impact to the Organization:
50%	1,000	$ -	$ 4,000,000	$ -
51%	1,020	$ 24,000	$ 4,024,000	$ 3,000,000
52%	1,040	$ 48,000	$ 4,048,000	$ 6,000,000
53%	1,060	$ 72,000	$ 4,072,000	$ 9,000,000
54%	1,080	$ 96,000	$ 4,096,000	$ 12,000,000
55%	1,100	$ 120,000	$ 4,120,000	$ 15,000,000
56%	1,120	$ 144,000	$ 4,144,000	$ 18,000,000
57%	1,140	$ 168,000	$ 4,168,000	$ 21,000,000
58%	1,160	$ 192,000	$ 4,192,000	$ 24,000,000
59%	1,180	$ 216,000	$ 4,216,000	$ 27,000,000
60%	1,200	$ 240,000	$ 4,240,000	$ 30,000,000
61%	1,220	$ 264,000	$ 4,264,000	$ 33,000,000
62%	1,240	$ 288,000	$ 4,288,000	$ 36,000,000
63%	1,260	$ 312,000	$ 4,312,000	$ 39,000,000
64%	1,280	$ 336,000	$ 4,336,000	$ 42,000,000

Of course, the scenario and ROI shown depends on two things: accurate measurement and changing behavior. Measuring time allocation anecdotally by asking reps or managers how much time they spend on selling is like trying to recall what you did every day last week down to the hour without looking at your calendar. It's guesswork. The most accurate way to understand time allocation, other than putting cameras on every rep, is to do statistical time sampling. This involves using a time sampling tool, like Sales Time Optimizer, to take random samples of rep days over a period of time (Figure 6-5).

Rather than attempting to audit reps like Big Brother, we want to create a communications channel for reps to tell us how their jobs are working and what could improve by looking at a statistical sample of days that we can analyze, understand, and use to take positive action.

From the reps' perspective, they log a sample day or sample week selected at random and submit it on the system. They'll log another sample day or week over the next couple of weeks or months depending on the sampling schedule and number of reps in the sample. From this information, we can create a granular picture of how the organization spends its time at several levels. The most fundamental is the categories of sales or nonsales activities. That cut alone will tell us how much sales capacity we have.

Figure 6-5. Sales Time Optimizer

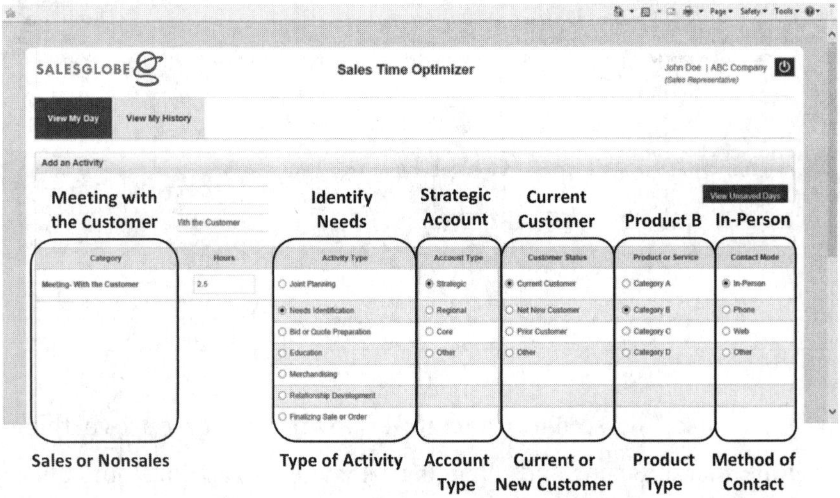

Going deeper provides more dimension. Activity type tells us what they were doing with their sales or nonsales time, such as identifying customer needs or attending internal meetings. Account type and customer status will tell us what types of customers the reps spend time with and whether the reps are doing new customer or current customer selling. We can also look at what they're selling, such as product category. Finally, we may be interested in contact mode. Are reps spending face time with customers or are they communicating by phone or web? Depending on the job, we may be surprised to find reps spending time on account management when they should be looking for new customers or doing internal work, and phone contact when they should be spending most of their time talking in-person with their customers.

We can use this time allocation to add another angle of visibility by connecting it with our CRM system and asking questions like "We know how many proposals we generate a month, but how much time do we spend developing those proposals and how can we make the process more efficient?" We can also look at our sales compensation system and ask, "Do our top quota performers and top earners spend their time differently than average performers and earners? And what can we learn from that?"

How willing are reps to share this information? Surprisingly, when reps understand the benefit of job decontamination and they understand that time sampling isn't monitoring their every activity, they're usually enthusiastic about participating and forthright about what they share. When the company takes action to make improvement, rep engagement usually strengthens because their participation has produced a benefit.

Changing behavior involves using time allocation data to provide statistical insight and make positive change in the organization. In addition to identifying contaminants, time allocation change can come from:

- **Eliminating activities that are not high value for the job or company.** For example, we may find that reps are spending time completing reports that have been a routine task for years—"This is the way we've always done it"—but are no longer necessary or valuable.
- **Shifting some tasks to a lower-cost resource.** For example, we may shift the task of taking inventory of our product at a customer location to a service role that's more efficient at that activity.

- **Leveraging technology.** For example, reps may produce customer proposals manually and that activity might be shifted to a proposal system. Our clients have found that the cost of systems like this can be covered in a short period of time by the sales team and the additional productivity and margin freed up by decontaminating the sales roles.
- **Changing how people work.** A client we worked with to measure time allocation found that their sales team was spending an average of only four hours a week in direct customer contact (Figure 6-6). Yes, these were sales people. They were supposed to be in front of customers, not in front of their desks or their colleagues. We asked what was happening. Over the time we had worked with the company we heard people from executives to sales reps talk about how they had a collaborative culture. It was a passion for them. But that culture translated to spending hours and hours a week in meetings collaborating . . . internally. No surprise, the result was lost sales productivity.

Figure 6-6. Distribution of Salesforce Hours

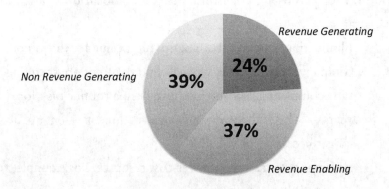

On average, direct customer contact time represents
only 49 minutes per day or only 4 hours per week.

The company was shocked when the lights went on and they saw the numbers that showed what their collaborative culture was costing them. Could they change the way they were being collaborative? The president took action and decided that internal meetings would only be conducted on Fridays. She went further and made it clear that she expected the sales team to be out in the market and, with the head of sales, set targets for sales time and customer contact time with the four days that had now been freed up. She also let the organization know that, because this was a critical priority, it would be perfectly acceptable to say no to internal meetings that couldn't be conducted on Fridays. Within a period of weeks, activity shifted dramatically; and over the subsequent quarters, sales time and sales results climbed, resulting in a record-setting sales performance for the year driven by changing how people worked.

Sales Capacity Lever #2: Workload

The second major sales capacity lever is workload, which refers to the time it takes to close a deal, whether it's winning a new customer or expanding a current customer. In sales capacity language, workload comprises the number of hours it takes for the average deal in the pipeline to move through each step of the sales process, the number of deals in the pipeline at each stage that require those hours, conversion rates at each stage of the pipeline, and the average time it takes for a deal to move from the top of the pipeline to close. Put all those pieces together and you can tally the time it takes to close one deal. This includes time spent on all the other deals the rep had to carry through the pipeline that didn't close. In the "Before" chart, tallying the hours for all prospects at each stage of the pipeline (given the conversion rates between each level of the pipeline) reveals how much total workload it takes to close one deal (Figure 6-7). For example, taking a sample of sales events, which are opportunities that hit any stage of the sales pipeline from qualification to close, provides valuable data to understand and manage the pipeline. A sample of sales events, when averaged, may show that:

- Of the 180 opportunities in the qualification step, each took about 1.5 hours to qualify for a total of 270 hours.
- Of those 180 opportunities, about 90 moved to the engaging qualified prospects step, where reps worked with those accounts an average of four hours each for a total of 360 hours.
- Of those 90 qualified prospects, about 45 moved to the creating proposals step, where reps spent an average of 4.75 hours each for a total of 214 hours.
- Of those proposals, about 15 are in the closing sales step, where reps spent an average of seven hours each for a total of 105 hours.

Figure 6-7. How and Where to Adjust Workload to Increase Sales Capacity

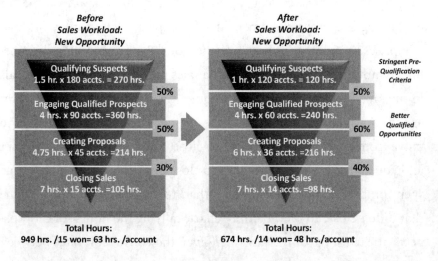

The total workload time includes all the hours spent on all the opportunities in the pipeline and totals about 949 hours in this case. But that

949 hours is to close 15 new sales. To calculate the workload to close one new sale, simply divide by 15 to arrive at 63 hours.

If we can decrease the workload to win a new sale or to manage a customer account, we can increase sales capacity because reps can close more new deals or manage more accounts with the sales time they have. We can look at creating a more efficient pipeline by examining our sales process and account management process and identifying points we can trim out or shift to other roles. For example, if we find that reps spend a lot of time generating leads, we may determine that it's more effective to shift that task to an outbound lead generation team. That team may be both less expensive and more expert at lead generation because they concentrate on and optimize that process as a team. As illustrated in the "After" chart, we could trim that pipeline by developing more stringent suspect pre-qualification criteria so reps spend their time on fewer suspects at the top. We may also create a more efficient qualification process that takes less time per opportunity. Those better qualified opportunities and our sales process improvements may increase our conversion rates to proposal. We may actually spend more time on proposals, with a better methodology that more directly addresses customer needs, which will increase our close rates. In total, those pipeline improvements can reduce workload to 48 hours per account, which substantially increases sales capacity, as shown.

Sales Capacity Lever #3: Talent

The third lever of sales capacity is talent—the people who provide the capability to sell and help the organization reach its goals. Headcount refers to both quantity and quality of the sales team. In the simplest terms, you can increase sales capacity by hiring more reps. For sales organizations adept at negotiating their quotas, headcount and quota bargaining is a regular practice. The conversation might go like this:

Nick, the CFO: "Jerry, your quota is $350 million. Jack [the CEO] has committed to the board, and this is your piece of it. I know it's a lot, but . . ."

Jerry, the VP of Sales (staring straight at the CFO): "You know Nick . . . you come to me with these unrealistic expectations every year. It's always too much, and we always have our backs to the wall. I give you the bottom-up on what we can do, and it's like you and Jack don't even look at it."

(Twelve seconds of silence that feels like two minutes passes as CFO Nick stares down at his wingtips, then looks across the room at the blank wall while VP of Sales Jerry maintains his unwavering stare.)

Nick, the CFO: "Jerry. I know. I know. We have to do this. You know the pressure we're getting from the board."

Jerry, the VP of Sales: "All right, all right. Look, I'll take the quota. But I have to add 15 new reps immediately. It's gonna take a couple of months for them to ramp up."

Nick, the CFO: "That's about five million in expense, Jerry."

Jerry, the VP of Sales: "I'll cut my bottom 5 percent of performers to make space and free up some expense. If you can get me the budget, Nick, I'll sign up for it."

The company wants more growth. You can push the current team to get more. They may be able to work harder, work smarter, find more time, or do more cross-selling of the product portfolio they have. You can add more heads, assuming the same level of productivity. But you don't have to. You can also upgrade your talent through training, development, or rehiring.

The first step is taking inventory of the talent you have. To understand your inventory, you have to understand what you're looking for in each type of job. Let's take a strategic account manager, or SAM, job as an example. What does a top performing SAM in your organization look like? What constitutes a SAM's top performance in your organization?

To answer these questions, first define performance and develop a profile of characteristics based on what top performers in your organization typically do or behaviors they exhibit. But doing this through subjective evaluation can be loaded with bias and lead to inaccurate results. We recommend developing a top-performing rep profile then evaluating your inventory of reps with a more objective three-point perspective (Figure 6-8).

Figure 6-8. Developing Your Top-Performing Profile

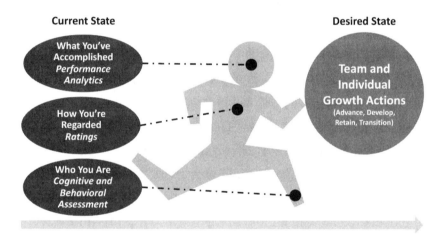

You can then use your inventory to take action by training your team according to a development road map and curriculum, moving people into roles that are a better fit (even if they're in the job market outside of your company), and upgrading your talent by hiring the right people with the right fit to be successful. Let's look at the three points:

What You've Accomplished—Performance Analytics

The litmus test for what a rep has accomplished is usually performance defined as attainment of quota, revenue growth, or profit growth.

Make sure you're looking at a level playing field when you look at sales performance so that it's related to a reasonable expectation (such as quota) and not just absolute dollar performance, which can favor reps with large existing bases of revenue or a book of prime accounts.

Analytics will give you a first cut at what a top performer in the sales role looks like. We'll usually look at the 90th percentile and above, for whatever performance measures are important for that role, as top performers. For a SAM, important performance measures may include performance to quota, annual retention of client revenue, penetration of clients through upselling and cross selling, and client profitability. If possible, look at multiple years and trends rather than a single year of performance data.

How You're Regarded—Ratings

For most companies, performance ratings are a staple of people evaluation. They provide an ostensibly objective way of evaluating people according to important criteria. The problem is that most performance ratings are actually subjective and subconsciously (or consciously) engineered by the managers conducting those ratings. Unless a manager has an issue with a particular employee, they will tend to rate employees toward the middle of the range. They may rate a few top performers toward the higher end of the range. After all, they want to be fair and performance ratings stay in the employee's file for years. Also, managers don't want their own teams to look bad. That could reflect on their performance as a manager. Before you send me an email about the great system your company has, understand that I'm making a generalization and not devaluing all performance ratings systems. A lot of companies have made it a priority to filter out subjectivity and develop effective performance ratings systems. The value in considering performance ratings is that they give you another view to correlate with performance analytics.

Who You Are—Cognitive and Behavioral Assessment

To round out developing the optimal profile and assessing your team, an assessment instrument can be valuable. Assessments typically use a set of survey questions to understand from the sales person how they would respond to certain scenarios (business and nonbusiness) and how they answer questions that test their cognitive problem-solving capabilities.

I find that a high-quality assessment tool can help create a picture of what a top performer looks like by displaying the characteristics associated with performance. For example, one of our favorite third-party assessment tools evaluates cognitive capability in the areas of verbal and quantitative reasoning and problem solving, much like a mini college entrance exam. For the assessment takers who have been out of college for years, this can create some anxiety. When I took it, I was thankful that I had recently tutored my daughter in algebra. However, rather than being an absolute in terms of right and wrong answers, the assessment is a relative indicator of strength in these areas compared to what a top performer profile looks like. This assessment also evaluates behavioral characteristics through carefully constructed questions to identify personality features such as assertiveness, attitude, decisiveness, and judgment.

Putting it all together, understanding how a cognitive and behavioral profile, performance rating, and the actual performance correlate for top performers gives you the information to develop the optimal performance profile for the role. At that point, you know what a successful person in each role tends to look like. While not without exception, these profiles give a good indication. Using that optimal performance profile can help you evaluate the profiles and performance of your entire team to take your talent inventory (Figure 6-9).

Figure 6-9. Creating Your Talent Inventory

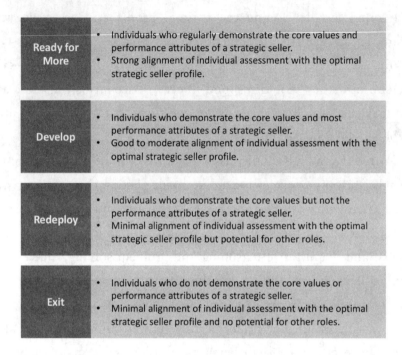

You can segment your talent inventory and take the necessary actions, which, as shown, may include:

- **Ready for More.** Take action by creating additional challenges and future paths for these high performers.
- **Develop.** Take action by training and developing this group according to a talent development curriculum.
- **Redeploy.** Find the right roles in the organization for these valuable players since they might not be the best fit for their current roles.
- **Exit.** Move these reps out of the organization because they're not a fit with the role or team. Note: Before taking action in this area, consult your human resources and legal teams to understand and follow the correct process for company policy and legal compliance.

Looking outward at the market, using cognitive and behavioral assessments as part of the recruiting and selection process can help you reduce subjectivity and error in the hiring process as part of upgrading the organization to increase your sales capacity.

Five Points to Consider

Sales capacity, the third dimension of the Quota Success Model, defines our ability to pursue the total addressable opportunity in our markets. While many executives may think of sales capacity as total headcount with an assumption on average productivity per rep, you can master sales capacity and use it to your advantage by understanding the drivers such as revenue flows, roles, time, workload, and talent, and focusing on how to improve those drivers to increase the organization's ability to grow. While you're calculating how you can hone your team, here are five points to consider:

- Understand your current retention, penetration, and new customer rates at the organization and rep level to know how you've grown and to plan how you can improve in each area.
- Build a dynamic sales capacity model to set the baseline of your current capacity and give you the ability to test scenarios on how to increase capacity.
- Determine your organization's current sales time allocation and develop an action plan to decontaminate and increase sales focus.
- Identify and create a plan to reduce sales workload for each sales team based on its mix of current account management and new customer selling.
- Develop the optimal performance profile for each role, take your talent inventory, and implement an approach to upgrade your mix of talent.

CHAPTER 7

Looking Ahead at History

My grandfather George was a pillar on my mom's side of the family. The Johnsons are a hearty stock from Sweden. George was in the first generation born in the United States and a carpenter like his father Ivar who emigrated from Sweden at the turn of the 20th century. Back then, a carpenter worked on the entire house, from framing to floors, and did it all without power tools. One year for Christmas, George gave me a toolbox that he had made. It was full of the things you'd expect to see in any toolbox plus tools we don't see today, such as a variety of handsaws and a brace and bit. No power tools. A brace and bit is basically a manual drill that would make my forearms and biceps burn before I could drill a hole through a two-by-four. It would prompt most men today to just hire a handyman.

George loved America, and he was a student of history. He read through history books and the classics and could quote verses and facts from memory. One of his favorite sayings was "nothing is permanent but change." But he didn't really embrace change. It was more comfortable to stick with what he knew. Another favorite phrase of his was "you can't tell what your picture looks like from where you're standing." He wouldn't have liked selfies.

One day at a Johnson family reunion, my family got a dose of how reliable history can be. We were down at the shore in Noank, Connecticut, where we had a few cottages. It was a sunny spring day, perfect for picnicking on the lawn by the seawall on Fisher's Island Sound. On the long porch railing of Aunt Thelma's cottage hung a 50-foot wide family tree with George's dad, old Ivar Johnson, at the top. Ivar was a card. When I was a kid, he was always joking around, even at an advanced age when he could barely walk. Near the family tree there was an old black and white photo of Ivar and his wife Anna about 80 years earlier standing near the same seawall where we picnicked that day. Ivar was obviously cutting up, sporting his Popeye-sized forearms (he was the one who taught George to use a brace and bit). Anna stood beside him, staring straight-faced at the camera with that traditional northern European seriousness, clearly not amused. We were about to hear another joke from Ivar, decades after he had passed.

My cousin Ronny called me over. Ronny had a past the family didn't talk about so I hesitated involuntarily. "C'mon down to the basement. I wanna show you something." I could only imagine what it might be as we climbed down the steps under the hatchway door into the musty space filled with items ranging from oars to crab traps. Ronny took me over to a box filled with books. He pointed to a stack of documents on top of the box. "Look. These are Ivar's immigration papers from when he came to the U.S. See . . . Ivar Johnson."

"That's cool, Ronny. Really interesting." I wondered why the papers weren't upstairs, displayed with all the other family memorabilia.

Ronny flipped to the next document. "Yeah. Yeah. But check this out. This one is from a couple of years earlier. He came to the U.S. before and then went back to Sweden to collect an inheritance and then returned. The immigration papers I just showed you were from his second entry into the country. This one is from his first entry." The name read "Ivar Anderson."

"Ronny! What?"

"Yup," said Ronny. "Ivar Anderson came over originally and then went back to collect an inheritance. He apparently was trying to avoid something—maybe the draft—and changed his name to Johnson when he came back to the U.S. We're all really Andersons, man!"

Years of identifying as a Johnson on my mom's side of the family instantly evaporated. "Should we tell everyone upstairs?" I asked Ronny.

So much for the infallible accuracy of history. Nothing is permanent but change.

Beyond the Historical

When it comes to quotas, most companies have a comfortable reliance on history. They use history as a rear-view mirror predictor of the future. After all, in a steady market environment, if we don't do much differently, we'll end up in about the same place next year, maybe with a little on top. But history is a terrible predictor of what can be done when we're intentional and aspirational about growth. That's why most companies that use history as a predictor in steady markets tend to plod along and most companies that use history as a predictor in growing markets tend to rise with the tide. But companies that want to outpace the market have to rely on something other than history to set realistic goals for future growth.

Quota Qualm: Can a Runaway Culture Use Quotas for the Wrong Outcomes?

Banking giant Wells Fargo found itself embroiled in scandal in 2016 after it got caught opening as many as 3.5 million unauthorized deposit and credit card accounts in a misguided effort to make an outsized sales quota. The bank paid a record-setting $185 million in penalties, more than 5,000 employees were fired, a number of board members were ousted, and the bank's reputation was tarnished. Another casualty: Wells Fargo's sales quotas, which were eliminated after the news broke. First reported by the *Los Angeles Times* in 2013, the scandal revealed that a personal banker working at Wells Fargo was expected to sell a whopping 20 products a day. "I am not sure how that's possible within an eight-hour day of work. Pretty much every customer takes an hour," Khalid Taha, a former Wells Fargo employee, later told the *Guardian* (Kasperkevic 2015). In 2014, the sales goal dropped to a still-unreasonable 15 products a day. According to Taha, a personal banker could reasonably be expected to sell only one product per customer. Fearing for their livelihoods, desperate Wells Fargo employees created fake accounts that they assigned to existing customers. Most of the employees who engaged in the scam didn't do it to make money; they did it to make a quota and keep their jobs. Quotas don't kill the organization, culture does. Look upstream from your quotas and understand what your organization is willing, and not willing, to do to attain its goals.

Most of the time when leaders set quotas, they're thinking about how to find a number that represents what a rep should be able to accomplish. The easiest way to predict this is by looking at past performance and making some assumptions around how much a rep should be able to improve. Leaders try to project a market's future by looking at what happened last year or over the past several years. The problem is that history alone won't give us any idea of what's possible. History has no view of factors such as untapped potential in current accounts, new opportunities in prospect accounts, competitive intensity, or market growth rates. Even looking at historical growth without doing the forensics about how we got there can be incomplete. For example, it's not uncommon to see a big one-time sale included in a rep's quota the following year, even though it's unlikely another major deal like that will come through again. With 65 percent of companies still using some form of historical method when setting quotas, this continues to contribute to quota attainment issues.

Historical quota setting can penalize high-performing reps by rewarding them with bigger quotas for the next year. With those new, bigger quotas, those previously high-performing reps sometimes fall short and underperform in year two. For year three, they receive a lower goal that more closely aligns with their lower year-two performance, then over-achieve that quota. The performance penalty cycle continues. It hurts both the rep and company.

When I think about performance penalties, I think about a beer company that we worked with. The company set quotas using historical methods. Because the beer business has a fast, transactional sale cycle at the level where the distributor sells to the retailer, the company used to set quotas on a monthly basis. Reps who did well on their quota would pay for it the following month with a bigger quota. The older reps shared stories with me about the newer reps—young bucks excited about per-forming well and beating their quotas.

A number of the newer reps sold a ton of beer, blew out their quotas, and got some great compensation in their first month. The old reps sat back and chuckled. "You know, just wait. You'll see what's coming next," they said. And sure enough, the next month, the newer reps ended up getting much bigger goals.

Over time, the newer reps learned how to play the game, which was to come in just at or slightly above quota, say at 105 percent. That way, throughout the course of the year, they could manage their quota and their pay. Compensation wasn't great, but it was pretty good and pretty predictable.

That's not the way the company wanted to motivate its reps. Unsurprisingly, the process ended up producing upswings and down-swings for some reps and an overall tendency for most to perform just around quota.

After examining the situation, we set up a process that removed the hard, monthly end points, incorporated market opportunity, and created a benefit to beating quota. The new process allowed the sales reps to exceed their goals and earn upside without the prospect of being saddled with a demotivating goal the next period.

I'm not suggesting that you disregard historical methods altogether. History is a valuable input when incorporated the right way in the quota process. There are numerous methods for quota setting, ranging from flat quota to indicators of market potential to account-specific opportunity planning (Figure 7-1). In the next few chapters, we'll take a look at several.

Keep in mind that the most effective quota setting usually combines two or more methods that fit the company's sales model, not any one method alone. And an organization may use different methods for different types of sales roles, accounts, and performance measures in the sales compensation plan they're setting quotas for. For example, the organization may use one method for middle market accounts, where reps have a large number of customers that need to be considered within broader market trends, and another method for strategic accounts, where reps have fewer customers and more information on opportunities within each of those customers. The organization may also use different methods based on the cadence and type of sales process.

Figure 7-1. Quota Methods Continuum

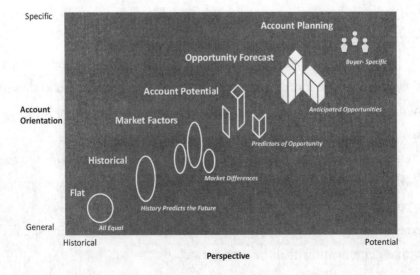

Quota methods range from historical general market views to more account-specific, sales potential–oriented views. Each of these methods is valuable in the right types of markets and sales models. While I've highlighted a few, there are others that are in between or derivations of these methods. But before we delve in, here are summaries of each method along with some of the benefits and challenges (Table 7-1).

Table 7-1. Quota Methods, Descriptions, Benefits, and Challenges

Method	Description and Application	Benefits	Challenges
Flat	Uses the same quota for each territory within a sales role. Effective for new offerings, standard offerings, new accounts, or new markets where each sales person has relatively equal market opportunity and equal sales capability.	• Simple and easy to understand. • All reps share the same expectation.	• Breaks down where territory characteristics vary. • If used for hybrid doberman and retriever roles, becomes obsolete as the current customer revenue base grows and revenue and potential vary across territories.
Historical	Uses historical growth trend. Effective for markets that are relatively stable from year to year without significant uncovered potential or changes in opportunity.	• Simple and easy to understand. • Good for territories with large numbers of accounts.	• Creates performance penalties where high-performing reps receive higher quotas based on their historical performance. • Encourages rep gaming to not overperform quota.
Market Factors	Uses historical growth trend and modifies that trend by differences in market characteristics of the territory. Effective for markets where specific account-level data is not available or reliable and where management has a good understanding of the dynamics of each market.	• A good hybrid of historical and market opportunity where reliable account level data may not be available. • Uses factors that are understood by the organization. • Usually seen as more equitable than straight historical method. • Good for territories with large numbers of accounts.	• Market factor evaluation relies on accurate management judgment. • Factors and method must be kept simple to maximize organization understanding and acceptance.

Table 7-1. Quota Methods, Descriptions, Benefits, and Challenges (continued)

Method	Description and Application	Benefits	Challenges
Account Potential	Uses indicators of account-specific indicators of sales potential, such as firmographic data, to estimate opportunity. Effective when quality account level data on revenue and indicators of potential are available.	• Provides valuable insight based on account-level firmographics that relate to sales potential (e.g., employees, white collar workers, technology spend, locations). • If field level data is acquired over time to build a more robust market database, it can give the organization a market intelligence advantage. • Good for territories with large numbers of accounts.	• Requires good-quality account-level data. • Robust and accurate data is often not available from third-party data suppliers, so the company must complement it with its own field intelligence. • Requires data analysis sophistication and an approach that can be simply communicated to managers and the field.
Opportunity Forecast	Uses historical retention, penetration, and acquisition data with an evaluation process to look at future potential. Effective for territories with a moderate number of accounts or when a moderate number of accounts comprises the majority of the potential, where account opportunity analysis can be conducted.	• Promotes discipline in CRM usage and forecasting accuracy. • Most effective if RPN (retention, penetration, and new customer) analysis is used as a foundation and supplemented with known pipeline.	• If only pipeline data is used, without considering historical trend or future potential, the method can be limited to the known pipeline. • Requires a disciplined CRM process to prevent rep sandbagging or withholding opportunities.
Account Planning	Uses detailed account knowledge about challenges, needs, objectives, and individual buyer needs to create an account level strategy that can provide information for setting quotas. Effective when the team works on a concentrated basis with a few strategic accounts.	• Provides a detailed view on each account that incorporates organizational and strategic dynamics not captured in market data or purchase data alone. • Good for a small number of strategic or global accounts that warrant significant concentration by the sales team.	• Requires the account management team to take a multiyear growth perspective on the account, rather than just looking at next year, to develop a challenging goal. • Sales leadership must separate the process of setting the goal from the process of account planning by focusing the team on growth aspirations and rewards.

Here's a look at the portion of companies that use each of these methods. Most companies will use more than one method and usually have different methods according to the types of accounts for which they're setting quotas (Table 7-2).

Table 7-2. Methods Used by Account Type

Quota Method	Percentage of Companies That Use This Method by Account Type (Most Companies Use More Than One Method)						
	Customer Segment				Current or New		
	Consumer	Small/Mid Accounts	Major Accounts	Strategic/ Global Accounts	Current Customer Accounts	New Customer Accounts	Total
Flat	6%	19%	6%	6%	16%	23%	42%
Flat Tiered	3%	17%	16%	10%	15%	16%	35%
Historical	0%	19%	42%	29%	41%	3%	65%
Market Factors	16%	32%	35%	39%	23%	32%	77%
Account Potential	3%	10%	15%	16%	6%	10%	26%
Opportunity Forecast	8%	23%	30%	31%	30%	26%	56%
Account Planning	0%	3%	26%	32%	13%	3%	45%

Let's start by taking a look at a few of the more historical methods that have a general market view.

Flat Quotas

With a flat quota approach, the organization gives all of its reps of a certain role the same quota. The 1992 film *Glengarry Glen Ross* gives you a good view of what flat quotas were all about. Blake (Alec Baldwin) wasn't looking at market potential. It was all about the leads and driving performance. Everyone had the same goal and was motivated to get the best leads and maximize their earnings. Well, third prize was "you're fired," so there were other motivators in play. Flat quotas can be effective for the right roles and markets. A few years ago, I worked with a sales leader in the United Kingdom who told me how he set quotas for his team of 20: "I basically take my growth goal and divide by 20." I cringed. Then I talked him through some other ways he might think about this since his 20 reps all had portfolios of customers that varied in size. Simply dividing the growth goal equally was unrealistic.

To use flat quotas well, you have to assume that all markets have approximately the same level of opportunity and all sales reps have approximately the same level of capability in terms of talent and capacity. It's a simple balance of the two factors we saw in the Quota Success Model: adequate market opportunity and adequate sales capacity. A good illustration is an industrial parts company I worked with a few years ago. They had a current account management team that was responsible for retaining and growing their current portfolio of customers. To set quotas for that team they used a complex method that looked at account potential. The company also had a new account acquisition organization, the dobermans, who pursued new prospects the company hadn't done business with before. They had about forty new account acquisition territories across the country. For quota setting, they simply took the overall company account acquisition bookings goal and allocated that equally across the territories. It sounds elementary for a sophisticated sales organization, but it was just one approach of several they used depending on the role. Why did it work?

First, because the market for these parts was large and not highly penetrated, there was an abundance of opportunity and no market opportunity constraints. The only constraint was sales capacity. The company could afford to put only a certain number of reps in the field. Second, the forty territories were well balanced and had about the same amount of greenfield, or new account opportunity. Third, reps didn't have an existing base of customers with varying amounts of current revenue and varying penetration, so that simplified quotas by only having to consider new opportunity. Fourth, all forty reps had about the same level of capability and experience since it was a role for reps who had worked in the business typically for less than three years. Fifth, because all of the reps had about the same level of tenure, their target compensation, comprising base salary and target incentive, was about the same, yielding about the same cost of sales with flat quotas. If any of these five factors changed—for example, if some markets were smaller than others with growth constraints, or if reps had wide ranges of experience and pay levels, changing target compensation and performance expectations—then flat quotas wouldn't have worked as well.

A variation on flat quotas is tiered quotas, which are flat quotas set at tiers within a role. For example, the company may set three tiers of flat quotas for the account executive role depending on the size of the geographic market each sales person covers.

Historical Method

Straight historical quotas assume that history is an indicator for future performance. Day-to-day life conditions us for this. We assume that we will do our jobs as well or better next year than we did them this year. That's usually a safe bet, right? Another example is looking at a prospectus for a mutual fund that cites last year's stellar performance and its track record over the past five years. We assume the fund will continue the trend. After all, despite the disclaimer that "past performance is not a guarantee of future results," the underlying message is that the mutual fund will continue on that path.

What's so different about quota setting? For one thing, companies that rely only on history, without looking at potential, tend to have fewer reps at or above quota and more sporadic "whip saw" rep performance to quota year-over-year than companies that incorporate forward-looking trends or indicators of potential in their quota setting. But history can provide a good foundation.

Kevin White, president of wireless and thermal systems with Laird, starts with historical methods and uses them as a reality check:

> Typically, it's a combination of market opportunity and historical trend. I don't spend as much time on the current pipeline, because I might have the wrong sales guy in place. What I'm trying to do is set a target based on the potential for a region or an area, not on what this individual can do. That's where I start. That's how I set for the fat middle. The market is growing and we're confident in this market, in general, it's growing at 6 percent a year, and, we've got about X share in this space of installed base, and a share of mind with customers in terms of engagement with the potential that's there.

Let's look at the straight historical approach because it can be a good starting point, a foundation upon which to build a more market-oriented solution (Figure 7-2). For example, a historical method may be modified or supplemented with other market factors, such as indicators of potential, to create an effective quota-setting method.

Figure 7-2. Historical Method

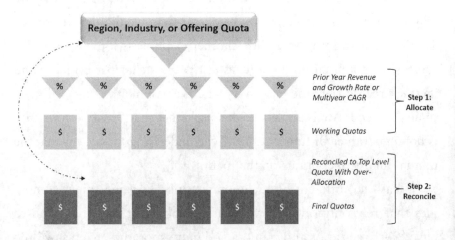

As shown at the top of Figure 7-2, the historical method starts with either the higher-level goal of the business overall, the region, and industry team; or with an offering or product team. As with any quota-setting method, if there is a top-down and bottom-up process, there are two important levels to note:

Step 1: Allocation. This is where the leadership team (such as the C-suite leaders of sales, finance, or general management) allocates the high-level goal down to the organization. Depending on the process the organization uses, the goal may be allocated down to a management level (such as region or district) or to the frontline level. Sales management typically takes those allocated goals (think of them as drafts or "working quotas") then comes back with its bottom-up response: "This is what we believe the organization can accomplish given its market opportunity and sales capacity." This top-down, bottom-up interaction is critical to getting alignment between the company and sales organization.

Step 2: Reconciliation. Once sales management comes back with its bottom-up recommendations, the leadership team usually looks at the numbers and realizes that they fall woefully short of the top-down number. (Well, I've never actually seen a sales management team come back with something higher than the top-down number.) This is the tying together of the top-down requirement with the bottom-up recommendation that we've talked about in other chapters. If there's a top-down, bottom-up interaction in the quota-setting process, then any of the processes that we've illustrated will likely have the two stages of allocation and reconciliation.

One client of ours, a global industrial chemicals manufacturer and distributor, uses a straightforward historical quota-setting process. They sell a portfolio of specialty and commodity chemicals mostly to large manufacturers and refineries around the world. Their two major business areas have different market dynamics and require different quota setting approaches. The specialty chemicals business is driven by innovation. The company and its competitors continue to develop new compositions to improve performance and meet evolving customer demands. Setting goals for this business requires a method that looks at potential on a micro basis from major account to major account. In contrast, the commodity chemicals business is stable and predictable. The major industrial customers tend to have similar levels of demand and grow on a predictable path from year to year. For simplicity, the company has used a historical quota-setting method for its commodity chemicals business and has applied more sales-potential based methods that you see on the upper right side of the Quota Methods Continuum to the specialty chemicals business.

How Do They Do It?

The company uses a historical method to look at the prior growth rates of each of its territories as well as the current share of the business that each territory represents, then uses that information to project ahead to estimate performance for the next year. For example, for each territory, the company takes three steps:

1. **Determine historical growth rate.** Look at the three-year growth rate of the territory and take an average of that growth rate, weighting the more recent years more heavily in that average. For the company, this gives a measure of growth for the territory.

2. **Identify the portion of the total business.** Look at the percentage of the total sales of the business that territory represented over the prior three years. For the company, this gives an estimate of how the territory compares to the rest of the business and gives some calibration to any overall changes to the territory's size or the size of the business.

3. **Calculate a blended rate.** Blend the territory growth rate and the territory representation within the business to create a growth percentage to apply to the territory for next year's goal.

Admittedly, this is an imperfect method for quota setting, but again, an approach that's widely used across companies. The historical method can also be approached in other ways. Some companies look at the most recent year's sales; others take a longer look back beyond three years. Some incorporate the weighting of the territory within the overall business. It's also common to look at the Compound Annual Growth Rate of a period of years and apply that as a rate to project forward.

While the historical method is pretty simple and easily understood, some of the challenges with historical quota setting include performance penalties in which high performing reps are saddled with bigger quotas as a reward for their high performance. Of course, one of the biggest challenges with this method is that it doesn't consider future opportunity or market factors that could affect growth. These challenges are a good segue to the next method, which uses history as a foundation then applies indicators of differences in potential.

Market Factors Method

This method leverages history to factor in differences in territories or markets that can make quota setting more future oriented. The beauty of this method is that it's simple to understand and apply, clear to communicate to the organization, and doesn't require detailed market information. It's a favorite of a number of our clients because of its practicality.

A company we work with in the energy consulting and services business uses the market factors method for all its account management roles. Because each account manager has a portfolio of customers and prospects, territory sizes and potential vary. One territory with certain kinds of accounts may carry a $7 million quota, while another territory with different kinds of accounts may carry a $9 million quota.

In this case, flat quotas won't work and historical quotas won't account for differences in opportunity over the next year.

Figure 7-3. Market Factors Method

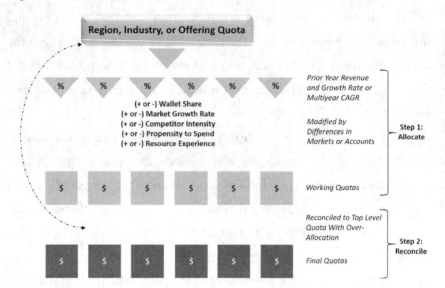

How Do They Do It?

To use the market factors method, the company takes the following steps:

1. Use historical information as a foundation. Start with a historical method in which it calculates the compound annual growth rate of each territory over the prior three years.

2. Identify market factors that impact potential. For each rep, apply a set of factors describing the difference between each territory and the region as a whole. For example, one of those factors is wallet share, the percentage of penetration the company has in that particular territory. If accurate information isn't available, the manager conducting the quota allocation estimates the relative wallet share in that territory. Next, the manager rates the wallet share in that territory on a scale from one (very low) to five (very high). Each level of wallet share has a clear definition to aid the manager with selecting the right level. Very low wallet share is below 20 percent, while average wallet share ranges from 40-50 percent. If the territory has low wallet share compared to the region overall, that rep would get a small uptick in their historical allocation because low wallet share indicates that there is still significant potential in that territory. The company uses five factors to adjust the historical allocation (Table 7-3). It applies a weight to each measure, resulting in a weighted average of each of the ratings. Those factors are:

- **Current Wallet Share (50%).** The percentage of market share the company has in the territory compared to the region overall. Lower market share increases the goal. Higher market share decreases the goal.
- **Market Growth Rate (10%).** The anticipated growth rate of that territory compared to the region overall. Lower market growth rate decreases the goal. Higher market growth rate increases the goal.
- **Competitor Intensity (15%).** The level of competition in that territory compared to the region overall. Lower competitor intensity increases the goal. Higher competitor intensity decreases the goal.
- **Future Propensity to Spend (10%).** The anticipated spending levels in that territory compared to the region overall. Propensity to spend could be driven by the composition of industries or types of companies in the territory. Lower future propensity to spend decreases the goal. Higher future propensity to spend increases the goal.
- **Resource Experience (15%).** The level of sales capability of the rep in that territory based on experience, tenure, and competency compared to the region overall. Lower resource experience decreases the goal. Higher resource experience increases the goal.

Table 7-3. Applying Five Factors to the Market Factors Method

Weighting of Factor	50%	10%	15%	10%	15%	
	Aggregate on Individual's Business Measures					
Next Year Historical Baseline	Current Wallet Share (1 - Very Low, 3 - Average, 5 - Very High)	Market Growth Rate (1 - Very Low, 3 - Average, 5 - Very High)	Competitor Intensity (1 - Very Low, 3 - Average, 5 - Very High)	Future Propensity to Spend (1 - Very Low, 3 - Average, 5 - Very High)	Resource Experience (1 - Very Low, 3 - Average, 5 - Very High)	Market Factors Allocation
$ 16,075,800	1	4	1	4	3	$ 17,281,485
$ 18,524,800	2	3	4	3	1	$ 18,571,112
$ 15,450,000	4	2	5	2	2	$ 14,561,625
$ 14,945,000	3	4	3	1	2	$ 14,758,188
$ 14,664,000	2	5	2	3	4	$ 15,397,200
$ 13,905,000	4	3	3	3	5	$ 13,765,950
$ 15,150,000	5	1	4	3	1	$ 13,900,125
$ 12,320,000	3	2	2	3	1	$ 12,166,000
$ 17,280,000	1	4	3	4	2	$ 18,187,200
$ 12,720,000	5	2	2	3	3	$ 12,115,800
$ 151,034,600						$ 150,704,685

3. Apply weighted market factors to the goal. Combine these weighted factors together for all territories to result in an adjusted goal based on the market factors for the company. By testing the weighting of each factor and by testing the sensitivity of each rating (e.g., how much a rating of five increases or decreases the goal), the company refined this system to create quota recommendations that represented the characteristics of each territory relative to all other territories. After the company produces "working quotas," it compares the total allocation to the top-down requirement and extrapolates the numbers to align with the top-down numbers.

I illustrated one example of the market factors method with five factors. The method can be used with a different number or type of factors that are most relevant to the business and account base. For example, you may apply the market factors method with two or three factors, weighted according to their importance. You may also adjust the sensitivity of the factors to give the one-to-five ratings more impact in terms of how they affect the historical quota.

When account-level potential data isn't available, we've used a creative twist on the market factors method: Look at the portfolio of the reps' accounts and rate each one on several weighted factors such as wallet share, competitive intensity, or propensity to spend. This takes the method from an evaluation at the territory level to an evaluation of accounts within the territory. Once you've completed the account-level evaluations, they can be totaled to the territory level for an aggregate view of accounts. Then refine the goal per territory across the business or region. For the account-level market factors method, look at all of the accounts in a territory or apply the Pareto rule to look at the accounts that represent 80 percent of the revenue and potential.

Through these first few methods, you can see that historical approaches work well in the right places and can provide a solid foundation for the first generation of market opportunity-based approaches. In the next chapter, we'll look at a couple of approaches that use primarily market opportunity to give a forward view on quotas.

Five Points to Consider

There are numerous quota approaches, but most can be classified into core methodologies that range from a historical to potential view and from general market information to specific account information. A company can use more than one methodology as long as each methodology is matched to the characteristics of the sales role, its market, and its performance measures. History is a natural starting point for many companies when they set quotas, but it doesn't provide a future view and can leave the organization basing assumptions on the past and thinking incrementally. However, historical information can be a valuable starting point on which to build forward-looking indicators of market opportunity. While looking ahead at history, here are five points to consider:

- Understand the range of quota methods and where they can be best applied by market and sales role.

- Triangulate in on the right method for each type of market and role your organization has, which may actually be a combination of methods.
- If more than one method works for a particular market and role, consider running each independently and comparing results and assumptions.
- Where possible, move beyond straight historical methods and incorporate indicators of potential.
- Make sure you push for simplicity in your method so that it scales easily and can be clearly communicated to and understood by the sales organization.

CHAPTER 8

You've Got Potential

The van ground to a stop just inside the subdivision entrance. It was a humid spring afternoon in Sarasota, and I was wedged in a vehicle packed with perspiring teenagers. When the side door opened, I scrambled to get out, walked to the back of the van, and hoisted my cardboard box of products to my shoulder.

Several months earlier, my family had moved south from New York and now, as the new kid in my high school, I knew no one. In that part of the country, most of the kids are friendly because many are transplants from the North and must learn how to make friends quickly. "They're just busy with their own friends. It'll take a little time," I assured myself. I didn't even have fake friends or haters because it would still be decades before teenagers would be plagued by social media. But it was sure better than being part of the lunchtime fights behind the gym at my old school in New York.

My parents got the brilliant idea that they could connect me with some instant friends by signing me up for a club. Since I had no particular interests that fit with the high school clubs, they found an outside group called the Junior Salesmen. They probably got a recommendation from their real estate agent, who was just trying to help on a topic of which she had little practical knowledge.

The Junior Salesmen's mission statement had a line in it about "keeping kids off the streets and out of trouble." They made us memorize it so we could recite it to potential customers if and when they opened their front doors. Being a pretty compliant only child, I didn't need much help staying out of trouble. Some of the kids in this group clearly did. I picked up some knowledge my parents hadn't anticipated as well as a few valuable lessons that lasted for years.

"Looks like a good one," I thought as I surveyed the homes in the subdivision. After months of walking neighborhoods with my box of cookies, candies, and other items people didn't need, I had honed my skills: I could scope out a good market and attack it efficiently. The high-end neighborhoods with the nicest homes, ironically, weren't the best opportunities. The residents usually didn't answer the door and, when they did, they had little interest. Since we could pick our neighborhoods, the newbie reps would usually go for those flashy subdivisions. I liked the neighborhoods with people walking around, with lots of cars in the driveways (suggesting hungry teenagers at home), with kids playing in the street—kids being watched by parents who could be easily persuaded to purchase an attractive box of chocolate chip cookies. Time of day was critical too. Late afternoon was a great time to swoop in on after-school appetites.

Without realizing it, I had learned to estimate market opportunity and to heat map—that is, quickly visualize—a territory. I knew nothing about sales. I just knew that if I could unload my box of product, I'd earn a few bucks and they'd let me go home. Understanding market opportunity was my key. And I was motivated.

❖ ❖ ❖

In the last chapter we looked at a few methods of using historical performance to predict the future and set quotas. Now we'll take a more forward-looking view at a couple of methods that are based on account-level estimates of potential and pipeline. Diane Boudreault-Owen of Plantronics describes the importance of understanding market potential and building specific intelligence on your accounts that you can't see with only a broad, outside view:

> I was in the solar high-tech industry several years back. The industry reports suggested that Hawaii as a market was the size of a pea, when in fact, we knew we were selling in a watermelon. And we were kind of like, "Shhh, don't tell anyone, we're going to sink the island with our solar panels, and no one will ever know how big that market is." And that's because electricity is so expensive there. It was this rich, open field that we were selling in. The industry reports hadn't caught up, and it took them years, because we weren't talking to them about this big market that we had penetrated. And therefore, if you backed up, and you looked at what the industry report analysts were saying, they kept saying to everyone, "Tiny little market, tiny little market." And the leading indicator that would tell you where your markets were growing had a lot to do with electricity rates, and no one was looking at it. And when we uncovered that gem, we could tell our sales force at large, go look at electricity rates, go mine those high–electricity rate locations, and go build into that white space. And so, that is intel that comes from the inside, from your sales team. It cannot come from an outside industry report.

Account Potential Method

As Diane Boudreault-Owen describes, the potential of a market may not be evident to everyone, even those who are well informed. Understanding the potential of your markets can give you unique, valuable information to inform your strategy and your quotas.

The account potential method considers firmographic characteristics across a large number of accounts to develop an estimate of the sales potential for each territory. These characteristics may include the number of employees, number of white-collar workers, number of company locations, and number of computers as well as office or plant square footage and other characteristics depending on the industry targeted and products sold. A company selling software to healthcare institutions may include the number of doctors at each hospital, physician office, or urgent-care facility as part of its predictive equations. By using regression analysis to identify relationships between the predictors and quota metrics such as revenue, bookings, units, or profit dollars, these market-opportunity factors can predict potential. Don't let the idea of regression analysis overwhelm you; it's actually a pretty simple way to determine factors related to or predictive of a buyer's potential to purchase your company's products.

One company, as an example, developed a method for estimating the potential for its products that was simple and easy to communicate to the field. The company, which is in the office products business, determined that the potential for their products was equal to about $1,200 a year per white-collar employee. Further, they were able to break down that $1,200 a year to about $550 related to consumable office supplies like paper and ink, $300 related to business machines like printers and copiers, and about $350 related to office furniture. With this information, the company could look across a territory of customers and prospects and get a good estimate of their total potential. Let's examine that example approach in a little more detail.

What Does It Mean?

Simply, in a given customer or prospective customer company, the total annual purchases of office products divided by the total number of white-collar workers averages about $1,200 a year. This calculation describes the potential of those accounts to purchase the company's products on an annual basis, not the actual purchase of any one account. Because these predictive relationships are originally calculated across a large sample of customers, they hold true across a large number of accounts at the territory and market level.

At the individual account level, however, the relationship of sales potential to white-collar workers might not be as accurate. That's because of the law of large numbers. (First demonstrated by the Swiss mathematician Jakob Bernoulli in 1713, the law states that as the number of trials of a random process increases, the percentage difference between the expected and actual values goes to zero.) As the number of accounts in a sample increases, so will the accuracy of the relationship between white-collar workers and sales potential. Also, since the white-collar worker variable predicts total potential, the actual amount of office products the company sells to any one account may depart drastically from the potential because, for example, they may sell only some of what that customer buys (say if a customer buys consumables from the company and business machines from another supplier). Or the account may not be a customer at all but a prospect that buys everything from the company's competitors.

How Do They Do It?

To develop an account potential estimation method, the company takes the following steps:

1. Identify indicators of potential. The company determines characteristics or factors that may be related to sales potential. This is a discovery step that comes up with customer characteristics that are externally identifiable and related to sales potential. Some of these characteristics are intuitive, based on what the company knows about its customers and prospects. For example, they look at total number of employees, number of employees at each location, total company operating revenue, number of company locations, company growth rate, and company industry. It's important to find factors that are externally identifiable; that is, the data on those factors should be readily found at the account level either from a third-party data source (such as a market research provider or the government) or from primary research on those customers. The company has to keep scalability in mind to apply this method across possibly hundreds of thousands or millions of accounts, so it has to identify factors that can be purchased for all accounts on a large scale.

2. Test and refine indicators of potential. The company applies the possible factors to a test sample of accounts for which it has good information to develop a predictive model. To explain this step and to prevent you from jumping ahead to the next section, I'll keep the statistics high level and make it easy to follow.

To determine the relationship between customer characteristics and sales potential, the company starts with a test sample of accounts for which it has high-quality information. The company selects a sample of several hundred accounts or more for each of its segments that are representative of the total market in terms of size and industry and for which it has good information on total annual purchase levels across all product categories. For example, the office products company has a good estimate of each account's spending on consumables, business machines, and furniture, either because it sold them most of their purchases in these categories or it has direct estimates from the account or field sales management on those purchases.

The company then identifies the relationship of each of the possible variables to the estimates of sales potential for the sample of accounts. The basic approach is to test each variable to see how predictive it is of total sales potential. So, the company might set up an equation with the total number of employees as a variable and apply it to all accounts in the sample. It might find that total employees alone have a relationship with sales potential. The measure of this relationship is what we call an R-squared, which is a measure of the correlation between the variable or variables in the equation and sales potential. So, an R-squared of 0.35 would mean that total employees as a variable explains only about 35 percent of what is related to sales potential, which is not a particularly good fit.

It might add another variable such as company operating revenue, together with total employees, to see if that combination produces an equation with a better fit to sales potential. As the company works through and tests combinations of variables, it may find that several variables are predictive, such as total employees and industry. It may also find that white-collar workers alone (which is actually a combination of total employees and industry) is predictive. The company determines white-collar worker count by examining a sample of accounts across industries and estimating the percentage of white-collar workers for each major industry group. For example, it may find that customers in industries like financial services have a larger percentage of white-collar workers than customers in industries like manufacturing.

While the company could use a more complex equation, it might decide to distill its equation down to a simple dollar relationship between white-collar workers and sales potential because it's easy for the organization to work with and easy to explain to the field. In that case, it would trade off any loss of accuracy for the benefit of clarity and organization buy-in.

3. Apply the predictive model to the full population of customers and prospects. With its predictive model based on the sample of known accounts in hand, the company next applies it to the full population of accounts in all its markets. It tests batches of accounts with the model to get a reality check from sales operations and field sales leadership on whether the model holds when applied on a larger scale. It also tests the model on a range of territories to make sure the sales team easily understands it.

Turning to the process as illustrated, the company applies the predictive model to all accounts in all markets to produce estimates of total potential. They also attach current sales to each account to identify the amount of untapped potential (above the company's current sales to the account), as illustrated in Figure 8-1. The company uses a combination of current sales levels, total potential, and untapped potential at the account level for each territory. It uses that information to provide bottom-up estimates of the opportunity in each territory and data that can be used to equitably allocate the top-down number by territory. The point I made earlier about the model being accurate on a relative basis is important here. While, in the case of the office products company, the sales team debated whether the actual potential estimates were accurate at the dollar level, they did agree that the potential estimates were accurate on a relative basis. While they may have disagreed that territory A had $25 million in annual sales potential, they did agree that the sales potential estimate of territory A relative to territories B, C, and D were accurate, which was what was most important for balanced bottom-up input and allocation quotas.

Figure 8-1. Account Potential Method

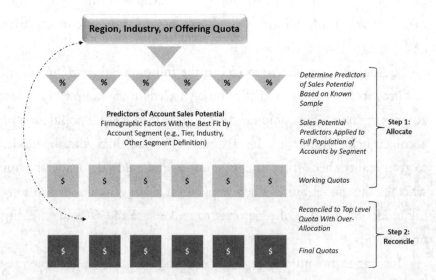

Breaking Out Sales Potential Estimates by Segment

The office products company example illustrates a simple approach that applies well to the market overall. For that company, a single view on sales potential worked well because most of its market tended to have similar demand for office products. Most of those customer and prospective customer companies tended to use office products in a similar way. They consumed them as most office workers do, regardless of industry. You might imagine a similar situation for companies such as small package shipping services and some telecommunications services that sell products and services that are used pretty much in the same way across segments. But what happens when a company sells its products to segments that have different applications and potential for those products? The sales potential estimation method in those cases may need to be more specific, based on how segments use those products.

We worked with a company that produces bar code scanning equipment and software. Its traditional market was the retail store segment that purchases its bar code scanning products and services for point-of-sale application at store checkouts. You certainly know this application from the multitude of times clerks have scanned your bottled water, beans, beer, and other grocery or retail purchases. In recent years, those scanning applications have extended to unstaffed checkout lines where you find yourself now doing the work (thank you very much) of the clerk who would have helped you and having to debate with a machine about why your avocadoes didn't ring up at the correct sale price. This bar code scanning company estimated sales potential for the retail segment by looking at data on the number of point-of-sale lanes in each of the stores in each of its target customers. With the advent of the unstaffed checkouts, the company could also look at the potential to help customer companies add point-of-sale locations that didn't exist before, in order to increase checkout capacity.

As the company looked at other applications for its products, they extended beyond the retail segment into industries that included hospitals (where bar codes are used for patient records), transportation (where bar codes are used on palettes and containers), and warehousing (where bar codes are used on palettes, cases, and boxes of goods). The bar code scanning company started with a broad sample of customers across industries (step 1 in Figure 8-1) to see what factors might be related to sales potential. Then the company sorted customers into logical groupings based on how they applied the bar code scanning technology. It found that it could define predictive models that were accurate for industry groups. Like the examples just mentioned, the company found externally identifiable predictors at the company level that included number of beds (for hospitals), number of trucks in fleet (for transportation companies), and total warehouse square footage (for warehousing companies). The set of predictive models developed for each target industry was more complex than what the office products company required, but it enabled the bar code scanning company to develop a level of market intelligence, market targeting, and quota-setting data that significantly increased its planning accuracy.

To recap, the account potential method:

- is effective when quality account-level data on revenue and indicators of potential are available
- provides valuable insight based on account-level firmographics that relate to sales potential (such as employees, white-collar workers, technology spending, locations)
- can give the organization a market intelligence advantage if field-level data are acquired over time to build a more robust market database

- is good for territories with large numbers of accounts
- may require the company to provide its own field intelligence if accurate data are not available from third-party data suppliers
- demands data-analysis sophistication and an approach that can be simply communicated to managers and the field.

Quota Qualm: When Quotas Become Bets That Are Too Big to Fail

In 1976, Continental Illinois Bank's chairman made a bold announcement: within five years, he promised, the bank's lending would match that of any bank in the nation. The scramble to achieve this aggressive goal prompted Continental to change its strategy away from conservative corporate financing. To make their number, Continental officers began buying up very risky loans made by smaller banks. Also, the bank got involved with dicey energy-related loans and investments in developing nations (right in time for Mexico's 1982 default and a subsequent debt crisis). Had those risks panned out, Continental would have become a powerhouse. Unfortunately, in addition to the foreign debt crisis, many of the high-risk borrowers defaulted. Ultimately, in 1984, the government had to bail out the bank—the largest bailout in U.S. history until the 2007-08 crisis. Continental was seized by the FDIC and sold to Bank of America.

This misadventure in goal setting—which gave rise to the expression "too big to fail"—should remind us that overly ambitious goals may lead to high-risk behavior and threaten the organization's very existence. Set quotas that stretch without betting the bank.

Opportunity Forecast Method

We need to regularly test our assumptions on market opportunity and the drivers behind it for current and new offers and markets. Kevin White of Laird recounts that type of situation:

In the controls business, which is safety critical, we were entering a new space—wireless safety systems, effectively a wireless e-stop like the red button that you would hit in a factory, emergency stop, to stop a line. You can wear it on your hip and walk around the factory with it. We thought that the product was going to be a big safety play, that you'd be able to shut down a line or a trouble area faster, and that would create a safer situation potentially for employees working there. So, that was the initial value prop.

What we actually found was that what customers were most interested in was productivity. If you're able to stop, let's say, a stamping line that's doing door panels for automobiles, you're able to shut that down two seconds faster than if you ran to the line. Now, it's not the safety, it's the scrap, it's the tool damage, etcetera, where the real money is. So, we would have been lucky to do less than half of what we targeted. We started to pivot, right, into the productivity value proposition [with our channel partners]. We triangulated on it. We took a look at a lot of wireless safety systems, interlocks, other analogous products—next generation, or nontraditional safety products. And from that, you can say, "Okay, we could get to that, to that level of penetration, or half that level of penetration over the course of X amount of time." So, you have an installed base, number of installations, unit sales per year, take rate. So, there's a bit of that. And there's a lot of voice of customer.

In looking at sales potential estimation, it's important to understand how your products are going to be used by each market to develop reliable correlates, whether in the account potential method or in reliable forecasts in the opportunity forecast method covered next.

The opportunity forecast method incorporates historical sources of growth that include customer revenue retention, account penetration, and new customer acquisition at the territory level with information about each rep's known and anticipated opportunities (Figure 8-2). The pipeline build at the territory level tells us about the opportunities we anticipate coming over the next year and also gives us an indication of the gap we have to bridge in order to reach the goal in each territory. This method is effective for territories with a moderate number of accounts or with a moderate number of accounts comprising the majority of the potential. The number of accounts should be manageable enough so account opportunity analysis at the account level can be easily conducted. For many companies, this would be 50 to 75 accounts per territory.

The foundational approach is to use historical information on RPN (retention, penetration, and new customer selling), which was described in detail in chapter 6. To recap, these three sources of revenue will provide a baseline of how we've grown in each territory in terms of:

- **customer revenue retention:** protecting the revenue we have from our current customers
- **customer revenue penetration:** selling more to current or new buyers in the account, or selling additional products to the same buyers in the account
- **new customer revenue:** winning new customers with whom we haven't done business before.

Looking only at the pipeline view without the foundational RPN gives us only half the story. It shows us the rep's or manager's view of what they think is possible. This will fall short of goal for at least two reasons. First, looking into the next year, we have limited visibility on the possible opportunities because we have limited knowledge and a limited time horizon about what we'll generate in the future. One sales leader we work with describes it: "With our business, our reps have to get comfortable with the fact that they can have visibility on only about 40 percent of their opportunities and that the other 60 percent will be generated by them, by partners, and by marketing. This happens consistently every year." The second reason the pipeline view will fall short is because most reps and managers will tend to underestimate what they think is possible, particularly when it's related to their goal. This can range from simply being conservative to outright sandbagging, where the rep omits known, high-probability opportunities.

When working with retention, penetration, and new customer acquisition data, we're not just using the historical information to build the quota. Rather, we're asking questions about what we anticipate will happen in R, P, and N next year—and why it will happen. For example, if the territory had 80 percent customer revenue retention for the most recent year, we'll ask why that happened, whether there were major customer losses that we don't expect to recur next year, and whether and why we anticipate improving our customer revenue retention performance. By combining the pipeline opportunity build with the bigger view on retention, penetration, and acquisition, we can create a picture of what's possible in each territory, which will help us to more accurately allocate quotas. Let's look at this in more detail.

A software and services company we work with used the opportunity forecast method for its major accounts segment, which was covered by an account management organization. The account managers were tasked with retaining and growing their customers as well as adding to the portfolio by winning some new customers each year. The company had previously used a historical method to set goals for its hybrid rep organization. For any shortfall between historical performance and the company goal, the company just spread the difference across the territories evenly without regard for actual potential. As we've noted in previous examples, this often results in sporadic performance and frustrated reps.

Figure 8-2. Opportunity Forecast Method

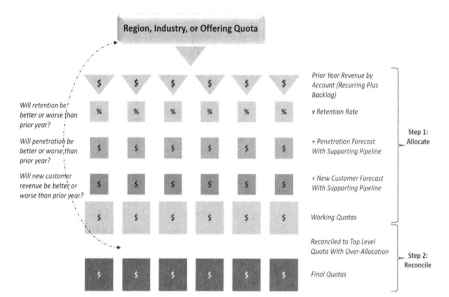

How Do They Do It?

Since this account management team had about 50 active accounts per territory, the company used a more targeted opportunity forecast method. Similar to the approach of the software and services company, the company took the following steps:

1. **Conduct RPN analysis at the territory level.** Using the method we described in chapter 6, the company calculates *how* the territory grew and its rates for customer revenue retention, customer penetration, and new customer acquisition over the past 12 months (Table 8-1). The RPN analysis alone provides valuable insight because sales leaders can dissect the accounts, wins, and losses that contributed to each component of growth for each territory.

Table 8-1. Retention, Penetration, New Analysis Calculation

Account	Year 1 Revenue	Year 2 Revenue	Revenue Retention	Revenue Retention Rate	Revenue Penetration	Revenue Penetration Rate	New Customer Revenue	New Customer Revenue Rate	Total Growth
Acme Services	$100	$85	$85	85%	$0	0%	$0	0%	-15%
Advanced Tech	$100	$115	$100	100%	$15	15%	$0	0%	15%
Allied Manufacturing	$0	$40	$0	0%	$0	0%	$40	100%	100%
American Central	$140	$70	$70	50%	$0	0%	$0	0%	-50%
Andover Holdings	$0	$12	$0	0%	$0	0%	$10	100%	100%
Applied Software	$120	$206	$120	100%	$85	71%	$0	0%	71%
Total	$460	$527	$375	82%	$100	22%	$50	11%	15%

R   P   N

2. Retention: Apply historical retention rate and make "why and what" adjustments. The company begins with prior year revenue for each territory as a baseline and applied the historical revenue retention rate. For example, as shown in the illustration using a sample of accounts, if a territory had $460 in revenue from the prior year and an 82 percent retention rate, the starting point for the opportunity forecast would be about $375 in retained revenue. From there, the company asks the "why" and "what" questions about the retention rate and makes adjustments to the forecast based on the answers to those questions. The "why" and "what" questions included:

- Was this retention rate representative of our average retention rate across territories? If below average, why was it low and how could it be improved? If above average, why was it high and what could we learn that we can apply to other similar territories?
- Were there any significant one-time losses that we would not expect to recur next year? Why did we have those losses and how can we minimize that type of risk next year?
- Would we expect retention to be the same, below, or above last year? Why?

- Based on the answers to the questions above, what is a realistic expectation for retention for this territory for next year and what should the retention number be?

3. Tally known retention or renewal opportunities at the account level. Identify gaps the rep in that territory needs to fill to reach that goal. This is the first step toward a territory plan to support the retention objective and attain the quota.

4. Penetration: Apply historical penetration rate and make "why and what" adjustments. The company begins with prior year revenue for each territory as a baseline and applied the historical revenue penetration rate. For example, if a territory had $460 in revenue from the prior year and a 22 percent penetration rate on the base of prior year revenue, the starting point for the penetration opportunity forecast would be about $100 in penetration revenue. From there, the company asks the "why" and "what" questions about the penetration rate and makes adjustments to the forecast based on the answers to those questions. The "why" and "what" questions included:

- Was this penetration rate representative of our average penetration rate across territories? If below average, why was it low and how could it be improved? If above average, why was it high and what could we learn that we can apply to other similar territories?
- Were there any significant one-time wins that we would not expect to recur next year? Why did we have those wins, and how can we apply that learning to similar territories?
- Would we expect penetration to be the same, below, or above last year? Why?
- Based on the answers to these questions, what is a realistic expectation for penetration for this territory for next year and what should the penetration number be?

5. Tally known penetration opportunities at the account level. The company identifies gaps that the rep in that territory needed to fill to reach that goal. This is the first step toward a territory plan to support the penetration objective and attain the quota.

6. New Customer: Apply historical new customer rate and make "why" and "what" adjustments. The company begins with prior year revenue for each territory as a baseline and applied the historical revenue penetration rate. For example, if a territory had $460 in revenue from the prior year and an 11 percent new customer rate on the base of prior year revenue, then the starting point for the new customer opportunity forecast would be about $50 in new customer revenue. From there, the company asks the "why" and "what" questions about the new customer rate and makes adjustments to the forecast based on the answers to those questions. The "why" and "what" questions included:

- Was this new customer rate representative of our average new customer rate across territories? If below average, why was it low and how could it be improved? If above average, why was it high and what could we learn that we can apply to other similar territories?
- Were there any significant one-time new customer wins that we would not expect to recur next year? Why did we have those wins and how can we apply that learning to similar territories?
- Would we expect new customer revenue to be the same, below, or above last year? Why?
- Based on the answers to these questions, what is a realistic expectation for new customer revenue for this territory for next year and what should the new customer number be?

7. Tally known new customer opportunities at the account level. Identify gaps the rep in that territory needs to fill to reach that goal.

This is the first step toward a territory plan to support the new customer objective and attain the quota.

As it applied the opportunity forecast method to quota setting, the company conducted the RPN and supporting pipeline analysis for every territory using historical revenue data and engaged the sales managers, and their reps when applicable, to work through the why and what questions and make refinements. The sales managers also evaluated supporting pipeline information for retention, penetration, and new customer opportunities to identify the degree of gap for each territory. With this bottom-up information, the organization provided input to the corporate goal and also used the information to equitably allocate the final corporate goal to each of the territories. As I mentioned before, with the pipeline forecast information the managers and reps also had a head start on territory planning to reach their goals.

To recap, the opportunity forecast method:

- uses historical retention, penetration, and acquisition data with an evaluation process to look at future potential
- is effective for territories with a moderate number of accounts or where a moderate number of accounts comprise the majority of the potential and account opportunity analysis can be conducted
- is effective for markets or business units where specific account-level pipeline and forecast data are available and reliable
- promotes discipline in CRM usage and forecasting accuracy
- is most effective if RPN (retention, penetration, and new customer) analysis is used as a foundation and supplemented with known pipeline
- can be limited if only pipeline data are used and historical trends or future potential aren't considered.

Five Points to Consider

Account potential estimation methods are a great way to look beyond history. As we saw in chapter 7, you can build upon history and modify with potential, or—as described in this chapter—you can estimate potential with the right data. It's important to start slowly when using potential estimation methods and lean toward simplicity rather than try to estimate with imperfect data and complex methods. The key is to provide visibility on opportunity while using a method that the organization understands and that can easily scale as the organization grows without requiring heavy manual calculation or administration. As you're thinking about your potential, here are five points to consider:

- Identify what drives sales potential in your accounts.
- Don't let a lack of detailed account-level data deter you but rather start with a first stage of simple assumptions.
- Build your base of account-level firmographic data as an ongoing exercise to increase your accuracy and create a market intelligence advantage for your business.
- Master your RPN analysis capabilities to understand how you grow in each territory.
- Use pipeline data to provide input to goal setting and a starting point for territory planning.

CHAPTER 9

Taking Account

A warm breeze picked up over the ocean as the waiter approached our table with the dessert menu. It had been a nearly perfect business lunch, if there is such a thing. I was riding copilot that day, observing my client, Paul, on a customer visit. He certainly picked a great location for this meeting. We were having lunch with Claire, the national head of retail sales for a major computer company.

The conversation had been lively and casual. We had shared stories, talked about Claire's business, and also discussed Paul's business. Paul had that regular guy look, not the profile you would expect for his high-stakes position. He was unassuming and approachable—the kind of guy you would walk up to at one of those chicken wing sports bars and ask about the score of the game. He would know the score and all the game stats as well. Paul did his homework, especially on his accounts.

As the end of lunch approached, Claire asked Paul in a friendly tone, "So, what can I do for you, Paul?"

"A golden opportunity," I thought. "Go for it, Paul."

Paul paused. "Nothing, Claire. I'm happy we were able to spend some time together, and I appreciate you answering the questions I had."

"What?" I screamed silently to myself. If anyone was in a powerful decision-making position, this woman was. She could jump Paul 10 steps ahead in this account with one phone call to her team. How could he just let this go by?

Claire seemed unfazed by Paul's answer and continued chatting. Lunch ended with the expected niceties as well as a few follow-up steps, then we all departed.

On the ride back to the office I had questions . . . a few big ones. I stayed calm and summoned my best relaxed, professional tone. "So . . . tell me about what happened back there. The meeting was going perfectly, and she would have pretty much done anything for you. I mean, how long did it take you to even get that meeting?"

Paul's answer was more than insightful. "About six months. I had to work through a lot of layers," he said. "You see, I could have asked her for a lot of things, and it probably would have helped our company. But anything I could have asked for at that table would have been too transactional and changed the character of the relationship. My goals for this account are a lot bigger. The best thing I could have done with Claire was to use that opportunity to ask questions, then come back later with some great answers."

Wow. Well played. And Paul actually had spent the majority of that meeting asking Claire questions about her business. He asked what she needed; he didn't ask for what he needed. In fact, the whole strategy was built upon his account plan that he had been working on for some time. As Paul mentioned, this meeting was part of a series that he and his team had laid out and planned over the past year as they set their aspirations for the account and how they were going to reach them. They were going deep on the account, setting their goals, and partnering with their chief sales officer and the customer in the process. It was working.

Account planning is usually used for developing strategies to grow the company's largest customers or to create pursuit plans to win major new customers. Just as an account plan can create the road map for growing the account, it can also provide valuable information on the potential of the account that can be applied to quota setting.

Account Planning Method

With strategic accounts, global accounts, and major accounts that are large enough that a few make up the bulk of the potential and revenue for the rep or the sales team, we can get more visibility by focusing on the opportunity account by account. This is where the account planning method becomes valuable for bottom-up input to the goal and for a tactical plan on how we'll achieve that growth in each strategic account.

The account planning method gets into the granularity of each account and engages the account team in developing a strategy and goals for the account. The account team is typically the account manager, supporting field reps, sales leadership, and, if the account is large enough, functions such as marketing, operations, and finance.

A client of ours illustrates the account planning approach well: The company provides engineering and software development services to major corporations around the world. For years, they had set quotas based on historical information on their strategic accounts. Unfortunately, this information didn't consider the potential and unique opportunities to grow those accounts. As you can guess from our prior descriptions of historical methods, this led to spotty performance year to year. The projects the company sold one year didn't necessarily repeat the following year because they were major investments for their customers that didn't occur every year. If the sales team landed a large support center development project one year, that customer wouldn't repeat the same project the next year. They might conduct another type of project, or they might not conduct any new projects—propelling the sales team toward opportunities in other accounts.

As the sales organization matured, its approach to working with strategic accounts matured as well. It developed a living account planning process that used a consistent method and structure to build the plans and develop a discipline to keep the plans alive during the year, creating accountability and driving results based on action plans they developed for each account.

Soon the historical quota-setting approach began to clash with the living account-planning process. As the top-down goals came in for the strategic account organization, sales leadership and the account teams began informing those top-down goals and the allocation of the goals to each strategic account with bottom-up account plan information. The result was an iterative process where the account plans from each of the account teams became a component in the quota-setting process.

How Do They Do It?

In my book *Essential Account Planning,* I explored how to create a living account-planning process. Here I'll focus on one component of that methodology: goals and strategy. To use the account planning method, the company takes the following six steps to build the account plan and the goal (Figure 9-1).

Figure 9-1. Account-Planning Method

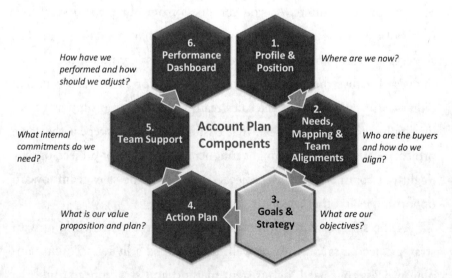

1. Establish the Profile and Position. The team determines where it is with the account now and historically. The profile and position component gives an overview of the account and the strengths and weaknesses of the relationships. It includes account history, competitive landscape, the performance of the customer in its business, and a SWOT analysis (strengths, weaknesses, opportunities, threats).

2. Map the Account Needs and Team Alignments. The team determines the customer's key team members, roles, and relationship strength. It then determines alignments of the account team to each customer member from decision makers to influencers. This component includes a summary of customer needs as an organization and individually, staffing of the account team, and identification of white-space opportunities where the company is not serving the customer but could.

3. Determine Goals and Strategy. At this point in the account plan, the team takes the top-down goal from the organization—usually a working goal proposed by leadership—and begins the "goal build" to identify opportunities for growth in the account. We'll delve further into this component under the goal build section. For each of the opportunities the team has identified, it creates a one- or two-page strategy sheet about the opportunity, the top challenge it addresses for the customer, the value proposition for that opportunity, and a summary strategy.

4. Create Action Plans. The team gets specific and develops a step-by-step action plan of short-term goals for each opportunity in the goal build that identifies the step, owner, and timing. The action plan puts the accountability into the account plan.

5. Identify Team Support. If they are to be successful, strategic account plans require resources. One of the most important resources is the team from the business that will engage to drive the plan. Team support can include the account team as well as other functions such as marketing, product innovation, operations, and finance.

6. Build the Performance Dashboard. The team determines the key performance metrics and milestones that attach to the action plan and to the ultimate goals in the account plan. The performance dashboard creates account plan and goal attainment visibility to the team and leadership and keeps the focus on attaining the goals in the plan rather than letting the account plan end up in a file cabinet until next year.

In total, these components bring the living account plan to life. A critical factor in the account planning and quota-setting process is eliminating incremental thinking about how the team could grow the account from year to year. For many strategic account sales teams, account planning only involves looking ahead one to three years and building a plan that could deliver single-digit growth. The team thinks about improvement over the base rather than thinking aspirationally about what the account could do over the next five to seven years.

With aspirational account planning, the team asks a first question: "What could we ultimately achieve in this account that would be significant for the customer and for us?" They identify a vision and an audacious goal that would change the value to the customer and how they're perceived by the customer, and would dramatically improve their lives as an account team (in terms of compensation, for example, or level of work, type of engagement, or competitive advantage in the account). Then the team asks a second question: "Over what timeframe could we achieve that goal?" They may answer something to the effect of "three years" or "five years." By putting their aspirational goal together with that timeframe, they create a trajectory to get there, which in turn prompts the strategy they'll need to get there. The second part of starting off on the aspirational track is to share that vision with the customer and begin the conversation about how the team can partner with the customer to provide the right level of value to reach that goal. In many cases, sharing the aspirational goal with the customer changes the way the customer thinks about the company and the account team and can reposition the relationship and help move toward a common goal.

Let's take a look at the goal build that comes with setting an aspirational goal for the account and that can be used to provide bottom-up input to quota allocation and create the foundation for individual action plans to pursue each opportunity.

Quota Qualm: A Less Deadly Catch?

Fishing the life-threatening Bering Sea for Alaskan king crab—a.k.a. "America's deadliest catch"—became safer and more profitable thanks to sensible regulations on crab-catch quotas. After the North Pacific Fishery Management Council and the State of Alaska imposed the rules in 2006, the industry saw only one death over the next six years—a dramatic improvement from the 1990s, which had an annual average of 7.3 deaths! Edward Poulsen, then executive director of Alaska Bering Sea Crabbers, a trade association, told CNNMoney that the industry, made famous by the Discovery show *Deadliest Catch*, did away with "fishing derbies," where crabbers rushed to fill their quotas in just a few days. "The gun went off and everyone scrambled," Poulsen said. "Some boats loaded too many crab pots and capsized. Others pushed their crews to work too long." During the derbies, everyone fished furiously until the entire fleet met its quota. Some boats pulled in hundreds of thousands of dollars' worth of crabs in a few days while others caught nothing. Fans of the TV show will recall 700-pound cages being winched aboard, swinging perilously close to workers and occasionally knocking someone overboard. Under the new rules, each boat receives a quota to fill during the three-month season. Quotas can be bought, sold, and even leased. Thanks to captains buying other crabbers' quotas, the number of boats shrank to 60 from more than 250 at its peak. Today's boats are bigger and safer. Plus, crabbers no longer need to go out during storms or work while sleep deprived. "Crewmen we surveyed said they're making about $100,000 a year and captains twice that," Poulsen told CNNMoney. "That's a lot more than a few years ago."

This fish tale reminds us that sometimes quotas are designed to set a pace, not create chaos, while making the business better.

The Goal Build

The goal build brings together the top down and bottom up. The top-down number for either the strategic account specifically (such as a global account that the organization is heavily focused on), or for a segment that comprises a number of strategic accounts, meets with the bottom-up estimate of what the team believes it can accomplish in each account over the next year.

The goal build identifies specific opportunities within the account that total to the growth goal. For example, the working goal for the account might be $8 million. The team expects about $3.5 million in retained revenue and backlog from current projects, leaving a gap of $4.5 million to grow the account. If the team only identifies $4.5 million in opportunities, it's probably going to be challenging to hit the goal; there would likely be some additional opportunities that appear during the year. But by identifying a multiple of that $4.5 million before the team gets the year started, it greatly increases the odds of hitting its goal. Of course, after identifying those opportunities, the team can choose to put them in its back pocket and not chance increasing its quota. But for most organizations, the quota setting process is healthier and more productive if it's open and based on a mutual trust that the team is aspirational in its planning and that the leadership is fair in its allocation of the goal.

If you are reading this and laughing about how this would play in your organization, that's OK. Brien McMahon, of Radian, describes the commitment his organization puts behind an open planning process to support pursuing big opportunities the team identifies: "We'll say, look, we'll bring the CEO to visit the customer if necessary, and/or I'll visit the customer. In other words, we will bring the aircraft carriers and help you secure that customer."

The team sets an aggressive multiple of the new revenue it needs to find and looks for opportunities that total, for example, three times that $4.5 million number, or a total of $13.5 million in opportunities that it will need to identify in the goal-build exercise (Table 9-1).

Table 9-1. The Goal-Build Exercise

Top-Down Goal	
Revenue Goal	$8,000,000
Retained or Backlog Revenue	$3,500,000
New Revenue Needed	$4,500,000
Multiple of New Revenue Target	3
Multiple of New Revenue Target ($)	$13,500,000

Goal Build	
Opportunity	Value
Partner Assessment	$1,120,000
Project Management Services	$680,000
Network Upgrades	$1,799,999
R&D Process	$2,600,000
New Product Development Support	$3,300,000
Launch Plan	$1,550,000
Launch Support	$750,000
Acqusition Integration	$2,800,000
New Product Requirements Definition	$850,000
TOTAL	$15,449,999
Surplus (Deficit)	$1,949,999

That $13.5 million is in addition to the $3.5 million of retained and backlog revenue. Identifying three times the new revenue is a task for most teams. The team usually works through the known opportunities—the easy ones that are on the top of their minds. They'll often come out about halfway to their three-times number. That's just flushing the lines of what the team knows about. If they hit their three-times number on the first pass, their goal may be low; that could indicate that too much of the bigger goal above the account is allocated somewhere else. At this point, the team begins the hard work of going through each division, business unit, and potential buyer in the account and referring back to the needs mapping in the account plan to start generating ideas.

When we worked through this exercise with our client's team, we easily reached about half the number. Then the team slowed down. So, we began to push their thinking. We took the problem statements or Challenge Questions for each buyer and broke them apart, looking for opportunities like we described in chapters 2 and 3. We asked about each opportunity from three perspectives:

- How could we work with the buyer in a traditional customer relationship as we had been doing?
- How could we work with the buyer alongside a partner who could increase our capabilities or access?
- How could we work with the buyer as their partner, co-investing in an initiative that was important to both companies?

After some discussion, the ideas began to flow. The team identified several projects that were on average larger than the ones that had come out in the first pass of flushing the lines. And this actually got them past their three-times incremental revenue number. With the incremental revenue number identified, the team was ready to provide their bottom-up input to the quota.

Five Points to Consider

The account-planning method is effective for sales teams with a small number of accounts that make up most of the potential and revenue in a salesperson's book of business. By using detailed account knowledge about challenges, needs, objectives, and individual buyer dynamics, it provides a comprehensive view not captured in market data alone. And, because it requires the account management team to take a multiyear growth perspective on the account to develop a challenging goal, it can help with estimating growth goals beyond next year. During your planning, here are five points to consider:

- Consider the account planning method for your largest accounts.
- Work within a living account planning process that creates regular visibility and accountability.
- Think aspirationally as the team is creating its goals and plan.
- Use the goal build exercise, in concert with mapping the needs of each buyer in the account, to push thinking and find opportunities that are a multiple of your revenue gap.
- Work with the account team and leadership to establish trust in openly developing the plan and setting realistic quota expectations.

CHAPTER 10

What's So Hard About Making Change?

I learned to deal with change at an early age. My parents were both frugal. My dad was a truck driver and my mom was a waitress at a local sandwich shop. They were World War II–era kids who learned how to pinch a penny. My mom described how, when she was in her 20s, young women saved money on pantyhose by cutting off the leg of a pair with a run in it and matching it with another pair with the opposite leg cut off from a similar run. Voila! A new pair of pantyhose.

My parents ran a tight ship. Whenever I asked for something for Christmas or for my birthday, they would listen. But there was often a change, unannounced. One year, I asked for a big boombox radio cassette player. I picked out exactly the right brand with all the latest features. On Christmas morning, my parents beamed as I opened up a big package, excited. Inside was a boombox. It sort of looked like the one I wanted but something was different. I learned later they got it at the pharmacy on sale for about half the price. They were very pleased about that. Two of the knobs wobbled because they were off-center but, if I turned it up loud enough, none of my friends noticed.

I really wanted a dog—a German shepherd like the ones on those police television shows. The day finally came, and my parents announced that Dad would be bringing the new dog home. The next day, I couldn't wait to get home from school. I ran most of the way.

When I got home, my parents beamed as an energetic dog bounded up and jumped on me. I laughed. But something wasn't right. The dog looked sort of like a German shepherd, but it was a little skinnier and had a brownish tint. I later learned that it was a Belgian shepherd. I don't know where they got it or why, but I thought maybe someone paid them to take it. I didn't say much. My parents were pleased. We named the dog Tiki because my dad had decorated our rec room with a Polynesian theme that was popular at the time.

The dog grew and turned into a hellion. Once I fed Tiki a can of dog food and, being a kid, I carefully placed the cylinder of compressed meat product vertically in the bowl expecting to watch him nibble away at it. Tiki swallowed the cylinder in one gulp. I was shocked. My dad installed a six-foot fence in the backyard to keep the dog in. Tiki learned to climb and jump the fence. My dad added wire mesh above the fence. Tiki countered by tunneling under the fence. I really liked my dog even though he was a little difficult. Unfortunately, several weeks later at dinner, my dad and mom broke the news to me that Tiki had tunneled under the fence again and run away. They didn't seem upset. He never returned. It was the saddest day of my young life.

I was talking with my parents about a year ago in my kitchen. We were reminiscing about the days in the old house when I was a kid. It took me about 40 years to get over the mental trauma and adopt my second dog. I remembered how much I missed that Belgian shepherd. I asked my parents, "Do you remember Tiki?" They both thought for a moment. "Yeah," my dad replied. "What a pain! He kept digging under the fence." He paused and took a sip of his drink. "We had to give him away."

"What?!" I was speechless. My parents stared blankly as they realized they had forgotten the story they told me. So much for managing change.

Change is easy to assume. We've finalized the new quota process and we're ready to roll it out. All systems go, right? Not necessarily. Remember the Challenge Question we identified back when we were doing the forensics and understanding the story behind the problem we were trying to solve? It involved people. People in frontline sales, people in management, people across organization functions. Now the change has to be put into action the same way: with people.

When we get deep into the calculations and the process, sometimes we lose sight of the human-change side of the equation. Effective quota problem solving and design should engage the team throughout the process, across the functions on your core design team (for example, sales leadership, sales operations, finance, marketing, operations, and human resources) as well as representatives from the organization who will be operating with the new quota process (such as field sales, strategic accounts, inside sales, and channels). So, when we reach the implementation point, the sales organization and teams using the new process have, at minimum, provided insight. They understand that improvements are coming.

To a reformed introvert like myself, sometimes all this change management and people talk can feel a little squishy. But there are some structures on how to approach change than can be valuable when introducing a new quota process or any other new sales effectiveness initiative. Let's take a look at some of the pillars of change.

Articulate the Why

If this sounds like we're coming full circle, well, it's because we are. We started the process by articulating the problem statement then redefining the Challenge Question. When we redefined the challenge question, we understood the story behind the problem, and we created a solution vision of why we would make this change as an organization.

Let's go back and bring that "why" to a higher level. The "why" becomes the vision and driver for the change. For example, if the organization was struggling with quotas that had a historical view, created performance penalties, and had little consideration of market potential, our driver might be that we have developed a quota process that's forward looking, considers opportunity in the territories, and sets the sales organization up for higher performance. The "why" should state the reason why the change is important for each level of the organization involved, from leadership to the front line. At each level, the "why" should be sharpened into a concise statement or message that will position the change. We'll pick up more on how to communicate this in your campaign later in this chapter.

Identify Degrees of Change

When we're making a change, it's going to be perceived by the organization in one of three ways according to how it affects them. For example, a sales manager may look at the change as:

- Positive: "It's going to simplify the way we're setting quotas." "It's going to result in less work for me." Or most important: "It's going to make it easier for my reps and for me to hit our goals."
- Neutral: "This is another new initiative. Hopefully it helps."
- Negative: "What are they doing to me? It's another corporate effort to sink their claws further into my organization. Getting the team to engage in this is going to be a royal pain!"

Some of these perceptions may sound familiar. Any of them could apply to the overall change or to parts of the change and have to be looked at individually. For example, "The quota process is going to make it easier for me to set quotas (positive), but getting the reps to trust it is going to be difficult (negative)." Take the overall change that you're planning and identify each change that each involved party (such as sales operations, finance, and front line) will see, and evaluate how that group will likely perceive it. Create a table that lists the changes, your evaluation, and communications actions you'll need to take to either address the negatives or promote the positives. Count the number of changes each group will see and determine whether you can reduce or simplify the number of changes. The changes and actions you identify will become content for your communications and coaching during the introduction.

I asked Tom Farrow from Charter Communications about these sorts of ratings. "If I am a rep in a room, I expect my quota to go up just because, to me, there are facts of life. It's not just taxes and death—it's that commission rates are going to go down, and quotas are going to go up," he began wryly before making a critical point. "But the quota doesn't go up if you don't put the marketing, the advertising, and the sales processes behind the scenes. What reps often don't understand is we'll have a $10 million productivity operation going on. And that is supposed to take the reps from being able to sell, let's just say, 10 widgets to 13 widgets over the next 18 months. Well, they see that as a 30 percent quota increase. And you have to sit down and explain to them, I mean literally, yeah, you've always done 10, as you saw this year, you did 11 or 12, and now that we've got all this in place, and we're doing this additional advertising, instead of 13, you're probably going to do 14."

Determine Readiness

I pointed out earlier in this book that managing change involves understanding and addressing the organization's tolerance for change and its capability to change. Tolerance for change can be driven by factors such as how frequently the team goes through changes of this type. The more frequently the team goes through similar changes, the more it may be ready and tolerant of additional changes. But beware: The opposite may be true. A team that deals with frequent change may become change fatigued and change averse. An organization that has gone for years without changing in similar areas may find even minor changes difficult to handle. We've all heard it before: "We've always set goals this way" or "We've never had quotas before. Reps determined their own objectives." The organization's culture can also determine tolerance. For example, some change-seeking organizations frequently challenge the norm while others are more inclined to honor tradition, even if it means being dysfunctional. Understand where each group affected by the change falls in the range of tolerance and how any challenges might be addressed.

The organization may be change tolerant, but it may not be change capable. For example, while sales management may be ready to take on the big change coming with the new quota process, they may not have the capability to conduct the work or the thinking required to provide insight on sales potential estimates for the accounts in their markets. They may lack the competency or the tools to make the process work. In these cases, understand where each group affected by the change falls in the range of capability and how any capability gaps may be bridged or strengthened.

Finally, the leadership team has to determine its commitment to change. Because change is rarely smooth and predictable, those who lead it will more than likely be confronted with obstacles to implementation. These could range from systems that can't handle the process that IT assured was possible to passive-aggressive sales and finance people who sounded like they were on board but who didn't actually want to deal with the change. When planning the change, the leadership team should ask itself, "How important is this initiative and what are we willing to do to make sure that it's successful?" The answers may range from, "It's important, but we don't want to push the organization too hard, so let's adjust if necessary" (the kids rule the household) to "It's critical to our success as a business and if we need to make some people corrections, we'll do it" (taking a firm leadership role). I can't judge where your team falls on the leadership commitment scale, but the team needs to be honest about where it stands before the changes start rolling.

Build Support for the Change

Prior to beginning the change, ensure that you've identified the people and infrastructure support required to enable it. Once the change is announced, assume there will be immediate confusion (either real or feigned) about how the process is supposed to work and what each person's role will be. If you begin with this assumption, you'll either find that I'm right or you'll be pleasantly surprised. One important support component is coaching to reinforce the messages behind the program and to teach and guide the participants through the process. Each year at Radian, Brien McMahon coaches his sales team through a process of articulating how they're going to achieve their new quotas. "Every year I get up in the sales meeting, and I talk about how we had a great year, a record year, and now we've got to do this," he said. "And you can see the faces in the crowd, they're like, 'Oh, we don't think we can do it.' And I joke every year, I say, 'You know what, last year, when I said this, you all had the same look, and we beat it by $2 billion. The year before that, you had the same faces, and we beat it by $3 billion. So, I am confident that we're going to beat it. And now, we just have to figure out how we do it. Let's go to work, and do it.'"

Coaching can also be valuable when conducted according to a developmental plan. For example, if some members of the sales management team need to develop their skills around goal setting or communicating with their reps, coach them on the disciplines and skills they need to strengthen. For sales, coaching may include getting granular on how to create a goal build.

For a new quota process, depending on the level and type of development required, coaching can be conducted by the sales operations team, the learning and development team, or by sales leaders.

Quota tools are also critical for scalability. One test for readiness of your new quota process is whether it can easily and accurately scale across the full organization. If the quota solution is so intricate or customized that it only operates in a small team environment with people who have a high level of skill around, say, analytics and quantitative decision making, you run the risk of the solution breaking down in full operation when it's subjected to sales managers or sales operations team members who lack the capabilities to make those decisions or run those calculations themselves. In that case, start working back through the solution to simplify and bring it back to the team's capabilities. A simpler solution that doesn't cover every aspect of market potential estimation or sales capacity but is within the organization's capabilities to operate is better than the most elegant quota solution that breaks down in operation. Systems can enable the operation of the new quota process by housing your methodology and process centrally in the cloud and enabling simple inputs from the organization and smooth, accurate calculations. I won't get into detail here about quota systems because that's a topic unto itself with considerable technical detail that's evolving quickly through a combination of standalone solutions and solutions embedded in CRM and SPM systems.

In terms of guiding principles, however, you should avoid generic "fill in your quotas here" tools and ensure that the quota system you choose or develop will work specifically for your methodology. The system should be able to integrate with your other systems and sources of information, such as account segmentation, territory management, and sales compensation.

When I asked Dan Lafond, Comcast senior vice president of national sales, about tools and methods, he mentioned the link between goal setting, compensation, and performance. "How can we make the people that are out there more effective?" he asked. "What are the tools, the technology that can make their job easier, better, faster? Compensation and goal setting is part of that, fundamentally. . . . So, if I'm a manager, I'm looking at the reporting, and say 'Katie, great job, you're 100 percent to your goals this month, but you're 85 percent to your commission target. Here's how we need to sell differently.' You have to show people how they can reach their goals, and you have to have the data and information to support it."

Quota Qualm: What Were They Thinking at the Veterans Administration?

The Department of Veterans Affairs set a system-wide performance goal of shortening waits for new appointments at VA hospitals to 14 days. Unfortunately, beginning around 2010, a tide of disability claims from soldiers who were injured in Iraq and Afghanistan created a severe backlog. When a VA hospital in Phoenix, Arizona, was found to have a waiting list averaging 115 days, the 14-day goal was put into employee performance plans. Big mistake. For a while, remarkably, it looked like the staff was nearing the new goal. Wait times were being cut—at least on paper. But as it turned out, the staff was fudging: Not all patients were being entered on an electronic waiting list, while other patients who had been waiting for a long time were simply purged from the list. In 2013, each of the 470 senior managers got performance ratings that made them eligible for bonuses. After a whistleblower alert and an independent investigation, which found that officials falsified records, the 14-day goal was removed from employee performance plans.

Aggressive quotas can drive dysfunctional behavior. Reinforce the right practices and back them up with analytics when making a significant goal change.

Create the Communications Campaign

Communicating the new quota process gets the message out to the organization in a planned way. Many organizations look at communications as a one-time event—and that's a mistake. They think they can announce the new approach to the organization once and begin working with the new process. But pretty soon they realize that the team didn't fully comprehend why the change was happening, or how they were affected, or what they were supposed to do. The result: a botched implementation that has to be repaired or relaunched. With most sales effectiveness changes, from quotas to compensation to CRM, you have one chance to get it right and build credibility with the sales organization.

We like to think of communications not as an event but as a campaign. There's a parallel to advertising: Think about those car commercials we see during the holidays with the attractive couple coming out of the house to find a new car with a big red bow on top. It's cute but it also gets across a message: "It's a great time to buy a new car and take on even more debt before the holidays and, if you do, your [wife, husband, significant other] will love you even more for it!" And it gets across that message over and over and over until you can't wait for the holidays to wind up just so those commercials will stop, at least for a year. The campaign approach builds on that concept but in a more positive way. Companies who implement and communicate effectively do it with a repeat campaign approach (Figure 10-1).

Figure 10-1. Communications Campaign

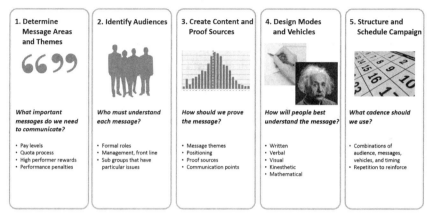

1. Determine Message Areas and Themes	2. Identify Audiences	3. Create Content and Proof Sources	4. Design Modes and Vehicles	5. Structure and Schedule Campaign
What important messages do we need to communicate?	*Who must understand each message?*	*How should we prove the message?*	*How will people best understand the message?*	*What cadence should we use?*
• Pay levels • Quota process • High performer rewards • Performance penalties	• Formal roles • Management, front line • Sub groups that have particular issues	• Message themes • Positioning • Proof sources • Communication points	• Written • Verbal • Visual • Kinesthetic • Mathematical	• Combinations of audience, messages, vehicles, and timing • Repetition to reinforce

As the campaign starts, you define the message areas and themes. For the quota process, this is where we bring back the "why" that we discussed at the beginning of this chapter and earlier in this book. The "why" includes the big messages the organization must know about the new quota process. For example, the process incorporates the potential of the markets, or the process levels the playing field for all reps to over-perform based on their opportunities. The campaign may also introduce a name or a brand so the organization can easily identify messaging about the new quota process. A lot of organizations will use this as an opportunity to develop a brand that's impactful and memorable.

Next, identify the audiences for the campaign. You may think of the audience initially as the sales organization, but a quota process is like any type of sales initiative: there are usually multiple audiences. For the quota process, audiences may include sales leadership, finance, marketing, field sales management, and frontline sellers. For each audience, look at your key messages and determine how those messages should be customized. The messaging for finance might be around improved cost control and planning for the return on investment in sales. For sales management the messaging might be around making quota setting easier and giving their reps better opportunities to perform.

Now that you've defined the messaging and identified the audiences, you'll need to create content and proof sources. This is the evidence that what you've said in the messaging is true. It's not enough to say to sales management that the quota-setting process will be easier. You'll have to show them how the process is simpler and takes less work. Similarly, you'll have to demonstrate why the process will give their reps better opportunities to perform. Maybe you can do this by illustrating how the quotas will be more balanced and aligned with market potential in each territory.

Modes of communications and communications vehicles are the tools that we use to get the message out. The most effective communications campaigns use various modes (the overall method such as verbal communication) with multiple vehicles (the medium carrying the message such as a webcast talk) to deliver the message over a period of time. People tend to respond to the modes that address the way they prefer to process information. If we introduce the program just one time via written announcement, a large portion of our audience (the people who absorb written communications well) will absorb it—or at least some of it. A portion of that group will actually remember and reference that information a month later (because recall fades and most people need to hear a message multiple times for reinforcement). However, if we leverage several modes of communication and communications vehicles on a recurring basis over a period of time, it increases the audience's understanding and recall of the messages by addressing their natural way of learning and processing information. Your portfolio of vehicles might include verbal announcements in meetings or small teams, email, company-operated website, company-developed apps, social media, or—depending on the company—old-fashioned bulletin boards. There are a range of communications modes and vehicles you can consider:

- written—for processing information through reading
- verbal—oral communications in large format, small group, or individual conversations to promote learning through listening
- visual—images and illustrations to simplify and communicate ideas through representations and relationships
- kinesthetic—activities and demonstrations to learn by doing
- mathematical—analytics and calculations for seeing mathematical relationships and logic.

Figure 10-2 offers a look at how reps across companies rate the effectiveness of a few vehicles. Direct, personal interactions in the form of meetings and one-on-one discussions rate the most effective by far with the all-too-convenient web presentations falling low on the list. The effectiveness of communications vehicles varies by organization, so determine what works best for your team and culture.

Figure 10-2. Communications Vehicle Effectiveness

Which Communications Vehicle Is Most Effective for Frontline Sales? (Percentage of Reps Who Rate Each As Effective or Very Effective)	
In-Person Meetings With Manager and Team	50%
One-on-One Discussions With Manager	31%
Program Documentation	27%
In-Person Presentations	18%
Leadership Meetings and Calls	17%
Job Aids, Apps, and Quick Reference Guides	15%
Web Presentations	2%

Combining communications modes and vehicles in the right blend (such as social media with written and visual components or an app with visual and kinesthetic components) will increase your vehicle's impact.

Finally, structuring and scheduling the campaign pulls all the pieces—message, audiences, content and proof sources, and vehicles and modes—into a cohesive campaign calendar that lays out the timing for the combination of vehicles that communicate your new program. At this point, you'll need to manage the campaign and provide a feedback loop for each of your audiences to ask questions and get support.

Five Points to Consider

We now look ahead to you making changes in your organization equipped with the tools in this book. I hope you've enjoyed the book and picked up some great ideas along the way. These ideas and tools are drawn from the experiences of many executives like you across a range of businesses; they're tested and practical approaches you can apply.

As you prepare for your change, remember that change management is too often overlooked by organizations that move ahead too quickly or that may not understand change's potential impact. However, they soon learn the value of effective change management and communications through the hard lessons that come with introducing a great program and expecting the organization to adopt it, only to see their investment fade away as the organization looks the other way. The biggest converts to change management learn that articulating the vision, engaging the audiences early, and taking them through a guided change process delivers great returns on their investment of time and resources. As you contemplate your change and look ahead to putting the tools in this book to work, here are five points to consider:

- Bring back the "why" of your new program to develop the big message around change.
- Evaluate how each group that's affected by the change will perceive the change in terms of positive, neutral, or negative.
- Determine your organization's readiness and capability for the change.
- Build support for your change with the right coaching and systems.
- Create and manage your communication campaign that includes messages, audiences, proof sources, vehicles, modes, and calendar.

Powerful Questions and Analytics for Understanding Your Story

Throughout this book, I've described various analytics to help you understand the story and articulate the vision for setting quotas in your sales organization. While the questions asked and the methods applied will vary from reader to reader based on their specific situations, we can all begin with a set of powerful, actionable essentials. Here are 10 of my favorite quota-related questions, along with analytics and suggestions of what they might tell you.

Question 1: How Is the Organization Trending on Performance and Quota?

Answer: Organization Performance and Quota Trend. This analysis shows the multiyear or multiperiod trend of revenue, quota, and quota attainment.

What to Look For: This is the big-picture analysis to identify issues that can impact the organization's performance. It shows the trend of three measures: revenue (or the primary volume measure of the company), total or average quota for that measure, and total or average quota attainment for that measure. It illustrates the relationship among those three measures and can indicate future direction. For example, in the analysis in Figure A-1, over the three-year period, average revenue per rep is increasing about 5 percent in total, although it is slowing. Over the same time period, average quota per rep has increased about 15 percent, perhaps in an effort to catch up with quota over attainment and continue to push revenue growth. Finally, average quota attainment has decreased. This suggests that the organization may have overcorrected on quota increases or that opportunity in the market or the team's ability to capture that opportunity has leveled out.

How It's Done: Plot total revenue or average revenue per rep with the multiyear period on the horizontal axis. Alternatively, if it's more relevant for the business, you can plot monthly or quarterly periods. For the same time period, plot average quota per rep and average quota attainment per rep.

Figure A-1. Organization Performance and Quota Trend

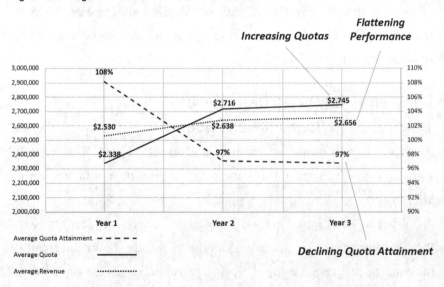

Question 2: How Is the Sales Team Performing to Quota?

Answer: Quota Attainment Distribution. This analysis shows the portion of the team at each level of quota attainment and highlights the percentage of the team at quota.

What to Look For: You should see a smooth, bell-shaped distribution with most of the population tapering off to 10 percent to 20 percent of the population in the high-end and low-end tails of the distribution with average performance for the team above 100 percent. A distribution like this will ensure that you're reaching the business goals within your planned cost of sales because your compensation program will likely be operating as planned for a normal range of performance.

Some companies still hit their goal by "getting there ugly" with an erratic distribution of performance that has a large number of high performers offset by low performance. On average, they get to the goal, but the large number of high performers triggers compensation plan accelerators, and the large number of low performers may barely cover their costs, resulting in a high compensation cost of sales. For high-performing sales teams, about 50-70 percent of reps are at or above quota in a typical year. Having a large portion of the team above quota also increases the likelihood that the organization will reach its goal and can contribute to a positive culture of winners as long as quotas are challenging.

How It's Done: Create a histogram like the one in Figure A-2, with groupings of percentage of quota attainment on the x axis. Typically, 10 percent increments provide enough granularity. On the y axis, plot the number of reps in each quota attainment grouping. Identify the 100 percent quota-attainment point to calculate the percentage of reps at or above quota.

Figure A-2. Quota Attainment Distribution

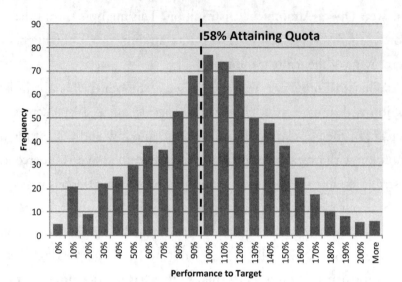

Question 3: How Consistently Is the Team Performing to Quota?

Answer: Year-Over-Year Quota Attainment Consistency. This analysis highlights rep quota performance consistency from year to year to identify whether there may be cross-year quota issues in terms of sporadic quota attainment at the rep level from one year to the next.

What to Look For: Each dot on the scatter plot in Figure A-3 shows a rep's quota attainment for year one (on the x axis) and for year two (on the y axis). For the sales team in total, a low correlation of year-to-year performance, or a shotgun pattern, as you can see, indicates that reps may have alternating years of strong and weak quota attainment. However, this doesn't necessarily mean that there's a performance issue. The highs and lows could be in the quota-setting method itself. To learn more, look at the next two analyses—Year-Over-Year Performance Consistency and Multiyear Performance to Quota Trend.

How It's Done: For each rep on the sales team, create a scatter plot that includes the rep's quota attainment percentage for year one on the x axis and year two on the y axis, as in Figure A-3. While you can see the dispersion of the pattern by eye, include the R-squared (described in chapter 8) for a measurement of correlation. A lower R-squared indicates a lower correlation between year one and year two quota attainment at the rep level. A higher R-squared indicates a higher correlation between year one and year two quota attainment at the rep level.

Figure A-3. Year-Over-Year Quota Consistency

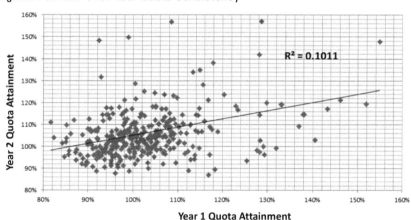

Question 4: How Consistently Is the Team Performing in Units or Revenue?

Answer: Year-Over-Year Performance Consistency. This analysis can be paired with Year-Over-Year Quota Attainment Consistency because it removes quota from the analysis to isolate rep unit or revenue performance consistency over time. Year-over-year performance consistency provides a clean look, without regard to quota attainment, at whether there may be cross-year performance issues in terms of sporadic unit or revenue performance at the rep level from one year to the next. Units or revenue can be replaced with profit dollars or any other performance measure.

What to Look For: Each dot on the scatter plot in Figure A-4 shows a rep's performance for year one (on the x axis) and for year two (on the y axis). For the sales team in total, a low correlation of year-to-year performance indicates that reps may have alternating years of strong and weak performance. As you can see, a high correlation indicates consistent performance between the two years. In this case, consistent unit or revenue performance, paired with sporadic year-to-year quota attainment, may indicate that the issue is with the quota setting, which may create swings in attainment from year to year, perhaps based on a historical quota-setting method.

How It's Done: Create a scatter plot for each rep on the sales team that includes the rep's unit or revenue dollar performance for year one on the x axis and year two on the y axis. As with the Year-Over-Year Quota Attainment Consistency analysis, include the R-squared for a measurement of correlation.

Figure A-4. Year-Over-Year Performance Consistency

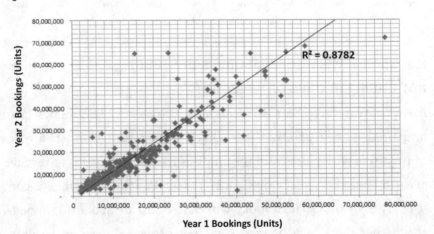

Question 5: How Are Our Reps Getting to Quota?

Answer: Quota Performance by Retention, Penetration, and New Customer Growth. This analysis illustrates how each rep or group of reps reaches their quota by retaining current customer revenue, growing current customers, and acquiring new customers.

What to Look For: Quota performance by R, P, and N can be valuable for identifying whether there are patterns of quota attainment in areas such as:

- **protecting but not growing**—high customer-revenue retention with nominal new growth
- **churning and burning**—high customer-revenue churn replaced by high new growth
- **concentrating on current customers**—focus on account management versus new customer selling
- **concentrating on new customers**—focus on new customer selling versus current account management.

While any of these patterns may be acceptable, they should align with the focus of the sales role and sales strategy. This analysis reveals valuable information about what's happening behind quota attainment that can suggest actions in terms of quota measures used or a shift in role focus. You can also look at other variations of this analysis that fit your business, such as quota performance by product type or quota performance by customer segment.

How It's Done: See Figure A-5. This analysis is a more detailed look at the RPN analysis described in chapter 6. Conduct RPN analysis as described in that chapter at the individual rep level. On the x axis, plot each rep according to their percentage attainment of quota. For each rep, indicate with a stacked bar the percentage of their goal that came from R, P, and N. For large sales teams, this can be complex to see

in a single graphical view, so you may want to look at smaller groupings of individual reps or a representative sample of reps. Alternatively,
you may look at the aggregate grouping of reps at various performance
levels; for example, 10 percent increments of quota attainment to see if
patterns exist at performance levels.

Figure A-5. Quota Performance by Retention, Penetration,
and New Customer Growth

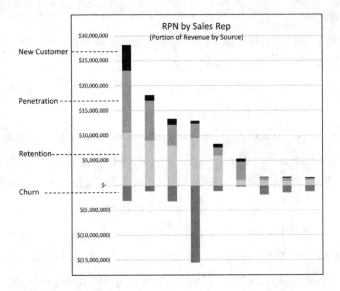

Question 6: How Consistent Is Sales Team Performance to Quota Over Time?

Answer: Multiyear Performance to Quota Trend. This analysis
tracks the trend of quota performance at the rep level over a period
of years at the rep level.

What to Look For: Performance trend concentrates on a sample
of reps that allows us to see patterns of quota attainment increases,
decreases, or sporadic changes over a multiyear period. These trends can
indicate issues with quota attainment, sales performance, or the quota
process. Sporadic year-to-year performance can indicate issues with the

quotas based on recent historical performance, while consistent downward trends may indicate increasingly difficult quotas or performance issues driven by talent or the market.

How It's Done: Create a trend line like the one in Figure A-6 for each rep in the sample that includes the rep's performance to quota on the y axis with each year shown on the x axis. An alternative look at this analysis is to compare rep unit or dollar performance trend to quota attainment trend.

Figure A-6. Multiyear Performance to Quota Trend Analysis

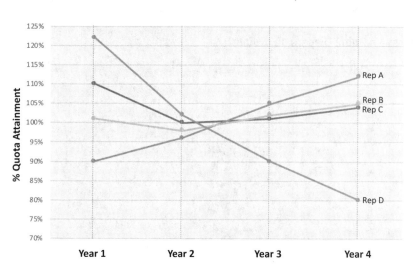

Question 7: How Wide Ranging Are Quotas?

Answer: Quota Dispersion by Role. This analysis identifies the range of quota levels within a job type to highlight the highs, lows, and frequency of quota levels.

What to Look For: For a sales role (account executive or account manager, for example), quotas should fall within an acceptable range. The exact percentage between low and high depends upon the business, but a wide range may indicate that the role is too broad. For instance, quota levels ranging from $5 million to $25 million may highlight that in this group the two different roles of account manager and major account manager are being played by reps. In this case, a need to create two roles is identified. A wide range may also indicate issues with equity or fairness. For example, sales managers may be putting greater quota burden on some reps while favoring others.

How It's Done: Create a histogram like the one in Figure A-7 with groupings of percentage of quota levels in units (that is, dollars or units) on the x axis. On the y axis, plot the number of reps in each quota level grouping measurement.

Figure A-7. Quota Dispersion by Role

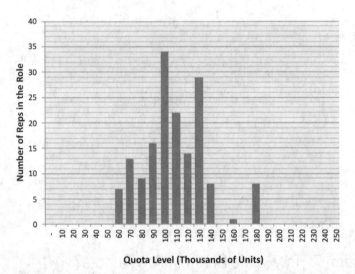

Question 8: How Do We Perform at Median and Where Should We Set Threshold and Excellence Levels Around Quota?

Answer: Upside and Downside Analysis. This analysis answers several important questions. First, where does the median or 50th percentile performer come in relative to quota and how does that relate to pay?

Second, where is low or 10th percentile performance and are we rewarding appropriately? Third, where is excellence or 90th percentile performance relative to quota and are we significantly rewarding it? The analysis is valuable as we consider how quota attainment relates to incentive pay and where we should position the high end or upside of the incentive plan as a percentage of quota as well as the low end, or threshold, of the plan as a percentage of quota. I'll give a brief explanation of how understanding upside and threshold levels relates to the incentive plan. You can go deeper in my book *What Your CEO Needs to Know About Sales Compensation.*

What to Look For: Each dot on the scatter plot on Figure A-8 shows a rep's performance to quota as a percentile ranking on the x axis. It's important to understand that this percentile ranking is not a percent of quota attainment but rather the rep's ranking on a scale of 1 to 100, which is relative to all other reps. Each dot on the scatter plot also shows a rep's incentive pay as a percentage of target incentive on the y axis.

So, if a rep has $20,000 of target incentive in their compensation plan and earns $20,000, then $20,000 of incentive earned divided by $20,000 of target incentive equals 1 or 100 percent on the y axis. Putting the two axes together, this analysis shows us a few critical statistics: As shown by plus sign 1, the rep at 50th percentile of quota performance is at 104 percent of quota, which indicates that a little less than half the organization is at or above quota. This distribution can also be confirmed with Quota Attainment Distribution (Figure A-2). Plus sign 1 also shows that the rep at 104 percent of quota performance is earning about 130 percent of their target incentive, which is handsome for performing just over quota. It suggests that other measures or accelerators are in the incentive plan that are increasing pay beyond the incentive for this quota measure alone.

Plus sign 2 shows the excellence level, or 90th percentile of performance. Reps at or above this level are the organization's top performers. According to incentive compensation best practices, we would expect that 90th percentile performance would pay 200 percent or more of target incentive depending on the industry and the company's margins. This example shows that the rep at the 90th percentile of performance is at 166 percent of quota; that's a typical range above quota in many sales organizations. It also shows that this rep earned a little over 220 percent of target incentive for 90th percentile performance, which is within a reasonable range for most organizations. Of course, we would want to confirm that upside incentive aligns with the actual design of the incentive plan. When setting quotas for the compensation plan, we usually want to determine the excellence performance level as a percentage of quota and this analysis helps us to identify the appropriate excellence level.

Plus sign 3 shows the threshold level or 10th percentile of performance. Reps at this level are the organization's low performers. According to incentive compensation best practices, we would expect that 10th percentile performance would be the point where the incentive plan begins to pay the first dollar. As I describe with the Reverse Robin Hood Principle in *What Your CEO Needs to Know About Sales Compensation,* the incentive plan should tip up the payout curve to not over-reward the lowest performers but to shift incentive pay to the top performers. This example shows that the rep at the 10th percentile of performance is at 70 percent of quota—not uncommon for many sales organizations. It also shows that this rep earned about 60 percent of target incentive for 10th percentile performance, which may be high depending on the design of the incentive plan. When setting quotas for the compensation plan, we also want to determine the threshold performance level as a percentage of quota. This analysis helps us to identify the appropriate threshold level.

Finally, this analysis gives us an R-squared that shows the correlation between percentile of performance and incentive pay. In this case, the R-squared of 0.7466 is a good relationship for incentive plans with more than one performance measure (for example, revenue and margin as plan measures).

How It's Done: Create a scatter plot for each rep on the sales team that includes the rep's percentile performance on their primary performance measure (such as unit or revenue dollar performance) on the y axis. On the x axis, plot each rep's actual incentive divided by target incentive times 100. So if a rep earned $10,000 of actual incentive divided by $10,000 of target incentive times 100, the value on the y axis would be 100 percent.

Figure A-8. Upside and Downside Analysis

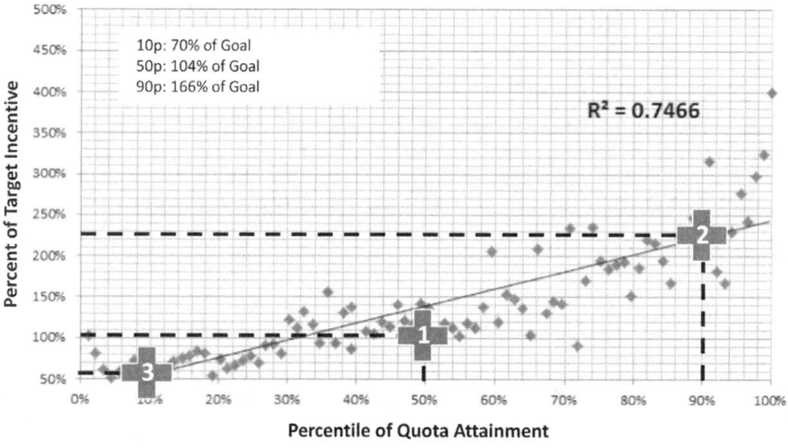

Question 9: How Does Performance Vary by Geography?

Answer: Performance by Geography. This analysis highlights overall quota attainment by geographies such as regions or districts.

What to Look For: For a sales role in a geography, this analysis shows the hot spots of quota over-performance or underperformance. It can help you quickly identify patterns in performance that warrant further investigation. For example, low performance in some geographies could indicate that quotas might not have been allocated effectively overall with some geographies receiving a disproportionate portion of the company's goal relative to market opportunity or sales capacity in that geography. Low performance may also indicate possible sales management or talent issues. This analysis is a great first pass to point you toward a deeper dive into some geographies.

How It's Done: See Figure A-9. Identify total performance to quota by geography and set parameters for green lights (100 percent of quota and above), yellow lights (90-99 percent of quota), and red lights (below 90 percent of quota). You should set your parameters based on your organization and roles. As an alternative, you can substitute total performance to quota for other metrics like average performance to quota, total revenue, or revenue growth. Using a few metrics like this will allow you to compare several dimensions within each geographic area.

Figure A-9. Performance by Geography

Team	Qtr1			Qtr2			Qtr3			Qtr4		
	Jan	Feb	Mar	Apr	May	Jun	Jul	Aug	Sep	Oct	Nov	Dec
Central	93%	95%	102%	82%	88%	87%	91%	87%	92%	78%	95%	92%
South	94%	83%	115%	79%	85%	84%	89%	83%	88%	74%	102%	95%
Midwest	120%	112%	108%	83%	97%	94%	99%	102%	100%	85%	91%	101%
North Central	82%	100%	97%	83%	84%	84%	90%	84%	96%	73%	93%	84%
Southeast	98%	80%	86%	81%	88%	89%	82%	85%	85%	84%	93%	99%
East	90%	86%	95%	80%	85%	81%	83%	79%	80%	80%	98%	98%
Appalachian	73%	90%	92%	82%	89%	73%	82%	86%	83%	81%	84%	84%
Southern Tier	82%	76%	94%	74%	77%	81%	81%	75%	77%	87%	100%	96%
Metropolitan	118%	90%	100%	88%	95%	91%	88%	84%	85%	86%	102%	109%
Mid Atlantic	92%	81%	88%	74%	77%	76%	81%	67%	71%	62%	108%	105%
New England	104%	101%	102%	83%	82%	85%	82%	77%	87%	82%	108%	103%
Grand Total	99%	103%	108%	91%	90%	81%	85%	81%	82%	80%	104%	98%

Question 10: How Does Quota Attainment Relate to Tenure?

Answer: Quota Attainment Versus Tenure. This analysis shows the relationship between quota attainment and the number of months a rep has worked with the company.

What to Look For: Each dot on the scatter plot in Figure A-10 shows a rep's tenure in months (on the x axis) and quota attainment on the y axis. For the sales team in total, the analysis identifies any correlation between tenure and quota performance, which is helpful to understand whether and how quotas should increase as reps progress through their careers with the organization. In the example, we see a broad pattern and little correlation overall, confirmed with the R-squared of 0.2968.

However, when we look at reps with six or fewer months of tenure, the pattern tightens. Further analysis revealed that average quota attainment for that group was about 40 percent, which suggests the possibility of a ramp-up program that could enable new hires and lower turnover in that group. One important variation on this analysis for organizations with reps who have high tenure is to consider total years of rep selling experience. This is because looking at tenure with the company alone can understate the experience of seasoned reps who were recently hired.

How It's Done: Create a scatter plot for each rep on the sales team that includes the rep's tenure on the x axis and quota attainment on the y axis. While you can see the dispersion of the pattern by eye, include the R-squared for a measurement of correlation.

Figure A-10. Quota Attainment Versus Tenure

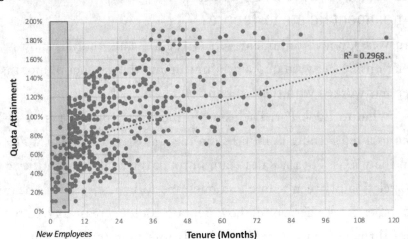

These questions and analytics are just a start. Think of them as tools to give you insights into your big questions, which can lead to additional investigation. Remember, work on articulating your Challenge Question, understanding the story, and conducting the analytics necessary to build out the story and your vision for the solution.

Acknowledgments

This book is the result of a lot of great work from many of my brilliant teammates, partners, and clients. Thanks to Louis Greenstein, my developmental editor, who helped me shape the narrative and bring the story to life. His expertise across numerous business books, including this second book with me, put a point on the message. Our SalesGlobe team provided motivation and input to make this a meaningful project. Michelle Seger, the big thinker, prodded me to develop the bigger "why" and to not just write a book about quotas but instead to write a book to expand the reader's ability to solve their quota problem through design thinking.

On our consulting team, Jim Benard, sales operations guru, tested my game to address the issues that matter to practitioners. Noreen Snellman, director of marketing, elevated our communications to the market to position the book in the most impactful way. Trish Burns, client experience manager, made sure we executed our logistics, from research to client interviews, with excellence and with the voice of SalesGlobe. Brian Street and Mara Lemmon brought practical application to help advance our thinking through great client work. Kim Boyd helped keep the machine running amid the project and research work always happening at SalesGlobe. Ron Cox, former client, fellow collaborator, and executive coach, counseled me over the years to think beyond the incremental, to grow over the long-term, and to bring this book to readers as part of the SalesGlobe vision of leading the world of creative problem solving for sales organizations.

To the ATD editorial team, thank you for taking the big step to bring this topic to readers. Thanks to Tim Ito for recognizing the idea from my divergent list of options, to Kathryn Stafford for her sharp editing that allowed me a lot of creative latitude, to Hannah Sternberg for bringing us to a strong finish, and to Carl Cox for teaming with me, as I revisited my art school days, to create a pure cover design with strong concept.

My family has been there throughout as I've invested countless hours in my day job as well as my creative endeavors. Thanks to my parents, Paul and Christina Donnolo, who taught me to pursue my dreams. Hopefully they'll forgive me for chapter 10. Thanks to my wife, Blythe, and my daughters, Isabel and Olivia, for being there through the thick of it all with love and resilience.

About the Author

Mark Donnolo is founder and managing partner of SalesGlobe, a leading sales effectiveness consulting and innovation firm. In addition to this book, Mark is the author of *The Innovative Sale, What Your CEO Needs to Know About Sales Compensation,* and *Essential Account Planning.*

For more than 25 years, Mark has worked with Global 1000 organizations on strategies to grow revenue. His experience spans multiple industries including technology, telecommunications, business services, manufacturing, financial services, and healthcare. Mark holds an MBA from the University of North Carolina at Chapel Hill and a BFA from The University of the Arts in Philadelphia. He has served on the Alumni Council for Kenan-Flagler Business School and Board of Trustees for the University of the Arts.

Index